Sharing the Gospel with Ease

Sharing the Gospel with Ease

How the Love of Christ Can Flow Naturally from Your Life

THOM S. RAINER

TYNDALE
MOMENTUM®

A Tyndale nonfiction imprint

Visit Tyndale online at tyndale.com.

Visit Tyndale Momentum online at tyndalemomentum.com.

Tyndale, Tyndale's quill logo, *Tyndale Momentum*, and the Tyndale Momentum logo are registered trademarks of Tyndale House Ministries. Tyndale Momentum is a nonfiction imprint of Tyndale House Publishers, Carol Stream, Illinois.

Sharing the Gospel with Ease: How the Love of Christ Can Flow Naturally from Your Life

For information about special discounts for bulk purchases, please contact Tyndale House Publishers at csresponse@tyndale.com, or call 1-855-277-9400.

Library of Congress Cataloging-in-Publication Data

A catalog record for this book is available from the Library of Congress.

ISBN 978-1-4964-6180-3

Printed in the United States of America

28	27	26	25	24	23	22
7	6	5	4	3	2	1

To Joe Hendrickson.
You shared the gospel with me fifty years ago,
but your impact on my life is eternal.
You introduced me to the Savior whom I serve today.

And always to Nellie Jo,
the true evangelist in our family.

CONTENTS

THE MOST IMPORTANT MESSAGE

The small town in Alabama where I was born and raised—population 3,700—had a disproportionate number of churches for its size. The churches represented multiple denominations, and a few had no attachment at all.

I knew of two Jewish families in town, but most of the rest, I think, would have identified themselves as Christians, though many were likely Christians in name only. My point is simply that there were plenty of Christians in my hometown who could have told me about Jesus. Maybe some did and I just don't remember, but I cannot recall ever having a gospel conversation with anyone.

Well, to be completely honest, there was one fiery young man from an independent church who told me on a few occasions that I was going to hell. But I don't remember him ever telling me how to get to heaven. But it might not have mattered. His caustic and superior attitude was an immediate turnoff, and I really had no desire to listen to him.

Most members of the denominational churches in town didn't talk much about Jesus. Obviously, I can't speak for every last one, but I can say that none of them ever shared the gospel with me.

Then Joe Hendrickson came to town.

Joe was the new varsity football coach at my high school, and he had a tough row to hoe. He was replacing a longtime coach who was greatly revered. Expectations were high.

To be honest, football was more of a religion than Christianity in that town, and there were two denominations: Alabama fans and Auburn fans. The definition of a mixed marriage was an Alabama fan marrying an Auburn fan. Many people wouldn't cross that line. One spouse would have to convert to the other side for the marriage to have a chance.

High school football was always in the shadow of the college game, but it was still important. It was very important. Joe Hendrickson inherited that rabid football environment when he came to town.

From the get-go, Coach Joe was in a no-win situation. The talent level had fallen off at our school, and most of the players and town residents still loved the former coach who had moved on. Coach Joe lasted two years in our town, and both years were extremely difficult for him. But those two years changed my life.

Though I hesitate to include this next part, I think it's important to mention another major factor in Coach Joe's story. This was in the late 1960s in the South, and integration had begun. African Americans, who comprised a majority of the population in our town, were slowly being added to formerly all-white schools. Racism was rampant.

A few African Americans at my school joined the football team, much to the chagrin of many families and players. But Coach Joe treated them like any other player. They got the same consideration, the same opportunities, and the same level of coaching as anyone else. It did not go over well with many of the townspeople.

I think it's important for you to know these dynamics because they form the backdrop for my experience with Coach Joe. In the eyes of the community, he had several strikes against him: He was new, he wasn't the former coach, and he treated everyone equally. And for that he felt the wrath of many people in town.

But Coach Joe did not let circumstances hinder his demonstrable love for Jesus Christ. What I remember about Joe Hendrickson is how his Christian faith just seemed natural. It was a part of who he was and it shone through in everything he did. I also remember how he willingly and eagerly shared about Christ with anyone who was willing to listen, including his football players.

I know because I was one of them.

To the best of my recollection, he called me into his small office one day after practice. I had no idea what he wanted. I feared I had messed up a play. But Coach Joe didn't want to talk football; he wanted to talk about Jesus. I'm sure there was a bit of small talk, but I don't remember that part. I just remember that he clearly presented the gospel.

He shared Bible verses with me that demonstrated that we are all sinners in need of forgiveness. He spoke powerfully about how God sent his Son to take the punishment for our sins through his death on the cross. He told me how Jesus defeated death through his resurrection.

And then he told me that Christ was offering me salvation and eternity as a free gift. He wanted to accept me just as I was. I could not earn salvation, but I could receive it.

Later that night, I repented of my sins and by faith accepted what God had done for me through Jesus Christ.

I became a Christian.

It has now been more than fifty years since that life-changing conversation. And however God has used me during those five decades, it all began with a gospel witness by an ordinary man, a high school football coach, who faithfully told me the Good News about Jesus Christ. God used Joe Hendrickson to set my eternal destiny to heaven.

What was so remarkable about Coach Joe was that he shared the gospel with such ease. And though I have since learned several different approaches to evangelism, I still remember how Coach Joe did it. He wasn't self-conscious and he wasn't trying to sell me anything. Our conversation was as natural for him as talking about a football play. Though it has become something of a cliché in Christian circles, Coach Joe really did speak from an overflowing love for Jesus Christ. Without a doubt, his joy and confidence in Jesus were clearly evident.

WHERE HAS EVANGELISM GONE?

Let's try not to complicate evangelism. At its core, it's very simple. Evangelism is sharing the Good News about Jesus Christ.

Two oft-quoted passages about evangelism—Matthew 28:18-20 and Acts 1:8—comprise what is typically called the Great Commission. Both passages capture some of the last words Jesus spoke on earth.

Matthew 28:18-20 tells us that "Jesus came and told his disciples, 'I have been given all authority in heaven and on earth. Therefore, go and make disciples of all the nations, baptizing them in the name of the Father and the Son and the Holy Spirit. Teach these new disciples to obey all the commands I have given you. And be sure of this: I am with you always, even to the end of the age.'"

Verse 18 is often omitted when this Great Commission passage is quoted, but it shouldn't be. It reminds us that we share the gospel under the authority of and in the power of Jesus Christ. Evangelism is not a human-centered effort.

In verse 19, where it says "go and make disciples," the verb *go* literally means "*as you are going*." In other words, we are to share the good news of Christ as we go through life—in every situation. As we go to the grocery store. As we go to the workplace. As we go around our neighborhood. You get the picture. We are to go with intentionality to people who are not yet believers in Jesus and tell them the Good News.

The point of sharing the gospel is to help people begin a *new life* as followers of Jesus. New Christians are to be baptized. New Christians are to be taught what it means to follow Jesus as Lord and Savior. And let's not miss the important last sentence in Matthew 28:20, which assures us that Jesus will always be with us.

In Acts 1:8, the other common Great Commission passage, Jesus is about to ascend to heaven. But right before he goes, he leaves his followers with this charge: "You will receive power when the Holy Spirit comes upon you. And you will be my witnesses, telling people about me everywhere—in Jerusalem, throughout Judea, in Samaria, and to the ends of the earth."

Once again, Jesus gives us a command that begins with a promise: The power of the Holy Spirit will be with us as we share the Good News. Again we are reminded that evangelism is not a human-centered or human-powered endeavor. It is the power of God working through us by the Holy Spirit. We are also reminded that evangelism is done with intentionality. We are to first share the Good News in our immediate surroundings, our "Jerusalem." But we are also to go beyond our immediate context and share the gospel wherever and whenever the opportunity arises.

So how is this endeavor going for Christians today?

Let me speak about my own context: North American congregations. In one study by our Church Answers team, we found that only one person would be reached with the gospel each year for every nineteen members in average weekly attendance. If you consider that most North American churches have only about half their total membership in attendance on any given Sunday, we can deduce that only one person per year will become a Christian for every thirty-eight members in a congregation.

If you find those numbers boring or confusing, let's simply focus on the central issue: *Most church members never share their faith*.

Jesus spoke of this reality to his disciples: "When he saw the crowds, he had compassion on them because they were confused and helpless, like sheep without a shepherd. He said to his disciples, 'The harvest is great, but the workers are few. So pray to the Lord who is in charge of the harvest; ask him to send more workers into his fields'" (Matthew 9:36-38).

Did you get that? Jesus is talking about evangelism. He is talking about the great opportunity to reach people. "The harvest is great," he says. But what's missing? *Workers.* People who are willing to share their faith. Jesus tells us to pray that God will send more workers. The opportunities are there, but too few Christians are willing to go into the harvest fields.

Such is the reality we find in many churches today. The communities where these churches are located offer many opportunities to share the gospel. But evangelism is not considered a priority.

I have personally conducted several hundred church consultations over the past few decades. Our Church Answers team has been involved in a few thousand consultations. The most common question I receive is this: *Why is our church not growing?* My typical response is that their church is not reaching people for Christ.

The next question they ask is also a common one: *Why aren't we reaching people for Christ?* Again the answer is just as simple: Because you aren't *trying* to reach people for Christ.

It's a sobering reality: Most North American churches are not evangelistic. And the churches are not evangelistic because their members are not evangelistic.

Yes, it is that simple—and that tragic.

The harvest is great, but the workers are few.

The message of forgiveness, the free gift of salvation, is the most important message in the world. And yet, as the church, we are speechless.

We have countless conversations every day. We utter thousands of words every day. We love to talk about our families. We often talk with great enthusiasm about our sports teams. We talk about the weather with both curiosity and concern. Yet we often feel our hearts racing with fear at the thought of mentioning the name of Jesus.

It's just not a natural conversation for most people. Silence is much more comfortable.

Why are we so uneasy? We will unpack that question in the next chapter. For now, it's important to understand that our silence plays into the hands of the enemy. Our silence is Satan's goal. He loves our hesitation, our self-consciousness, and our unwillingness to share the gospel. His goal is to increase the population of hell. Every gospel conversation is a threat to his dominion. This is spiritual warfare at its most basic level.

EVANGELISM AS SPIRITUAL WARFARE

"Resist the enemy."

Those words were written by the apostle Paul to the church at Ephesus. And though he doesn't mention evangelism by name in this passage, he pulls back the curtain to show us the true battlefield in the struggle to win human hearts for the Lord. Look at Ephesians 6:10-13:

> A final word: Be strong in the Lord and his mighty power. Put on all of God's armor so that you will be able to stand firm against all strategies of the devil. For we are not fighting against flesh-and-blood enemies, but against evil rulers and authorities of the unseen world, against mighty powers in this dark world, and against evil spirits in the heavenly places.
>
> Therefore, put on every piece of God's armor so you will be able to resist the enemy in the time of evil. Then after the battle you will still be standing firm.

Our enemy is evil. He has strategies to oppose us. His power is mighty in a dark world.

The challenge might seem too great were it not for the powerful admonition at the beginning of the passage: *Be strong in the Lord and his mighty power.* We have the Lord on our side, along with his all-surpassing power. In him we can stand strong in the face of the enemy.

When we are witnesses for Christ, we have the power of God behind us and the full armor of God to protect us. But when we are silent, none of that matters. If we *don't* share the gospel, if we come up with convenient excuses not to evangelize, we're simply giving Satan his way. Satan wants us to keep quiet. He is very comfortable with silent, self-absorbed churches.

Look at Ephesians 6:14-15: "Stand your ground, putting on the belt of truth and the body armor of God's righteousness. For shoes, put on the peace that comes from the Good News so that you will be fully prepared."

Did you get that? We have peace in the battle because we have the Good News. We can be fully prepared because we have the gospel. And because we have the gospel, we have the authority and the mandate to share the gospel.

Evangelism is the enemy of the devil. Evangelism is a God-given, Spirit-empowered mandate to share the gospel of Jesus. Those who hear and gladly receive the gospel message become citizens of heaven. They depopulate hell.

Evangelism is indeed spiritual warfare. It is the greatest threat to Satan and his dominion.

By the way, Paul wrote these words about spiritual warfare at the end of his letter to the church at Ephesus, right before his final greetings. He wanted them to be the last thing the church members heard when the letter was read to the church.

If this message was vitally important to the church in the first century, it is no less important in our day.

EVERY CHRISTIAN'S RESPONSIBILITY

My first year as a pastor, many years ago, was spent in a church founded in the late 1700s that had dwindled to seven members in attendance. I know beyond a shadow of a doubt that the only reason they called me as pastor was that I was the only candidate they had. If you had heard me preach, you would understand.

The first few months were a typical honeymoon phase. The church members loved me and showed it. I loved them as well. We had a nice period of growth as people in the community began to discover that the once-dead rural church had a bit of new life. We even saw some people become followers of Jesus, something that hadn't happened in that church in more than twenty-five years. The early stages of ministry there were really fun.

But the honeymoon phase always comes to an end, and this church was no exception. There was no big controversy. The critics were only mildly vocal. But the season of unity and laughter had waned. Its decline was noticeable and troubling.

As you might imagine, we entered another drought of seeing people come to Christ. The excitement of the early days turned to apathy. Old patterns of neglect, silence, and frustration reemerged—slowly but with certainty.

I once told my wife that I wanted to write a book on

mistakes I'd made as a pastor. Without missing a beat, she deadpanned her response: "It would have to be a multi-volume series." Well, I made one of those many mistakes early in my time at this first church. I used the Lord's pulpit as a bully pulpit for my own frustrations.

I don't recall the biblical text I used for this particular sermon, but in truth it didn't matter. I wasn't interested in explaining God's Word to the people. I wanted to fuss at them. I wanted to point out their inadequacies.

So I did.

I know I said a lot of negative things that morning, but the one specific point that stands out in my memory was telling the members they were sending people to hell because of their disobedience and silence.

I felt terrible after that message. Even if some of what I said was true, my heart was in the wrong place. I spoke out of anger and spite. It's no wonder I felt awful.

Not long after I gave that sermon, God convicted me of two major issues of sin in my life.

First, I had used the sacred time of preaching the Word to vent my own anger and frustration—wielding my sermon as a weapon rather than offering it as God's tool.

Second, I was convicted of my own spiritual inconsistency—my own lack of time in the Bible and in prayer and my own silence in evangelism.

I had preached harshly to my congregation about

evangelism when I wasn't even doing it myself. I shouted a message, but I wasn't living that message.

Evangelism is every Christian's responsibility, and it is certainly the responsibility of those who would lead God's people.

Don't get me wrong: If you're a church member and you're expecting your pastor and staff to do all the evangelism, your thinking is just as wrong as mine was when I berated my congregation for not doing more. Evangelism is not something to delegate. And it's not something to hire out. According to Paul in Ephesians 4:12, it is the responsibility of those gifted as apostles, prophets, evangelists, and pastors and teachers to "equip God's people to do his work and build up the church, the body of Christ." But it is everyone's responsibility to *do* the ministry, to pursue the Great Commission, to spread the Good News.

SHARING THE MESSAGE WITH EASE

Think about an incredibly joyous event in your life. Perhaps something as basic as your team winning a championship. Do you remember how you couldn't wait to talk about it? Do you remember your excitement and enthusiasm? You were willing and eager to have a conversation about your team with anyone who would listen.

I remember when I found out Nellie Jo was pregnant

with our first child. I had to tell someone. There was no internet in those days, but I couldn't wait to get on the phone and spread the news. If you're of a certain age, as I am, you remember how expensive long-distance calls were in those days. I didn't care. I had to tell people. I had to tell a *lot* of people.

My excitement was renewed with the same intensity for each of Nellie Jo's pregnancies and the births of all three sons. A couple of decades later, I felt a new excitement and eagerness to tell others about the arrival of each of my grandchildren.

The point is simple. When we are truly excited about something, we have to share it. We're not deterred by obstacles or worried about how we might come across. We just have to get the news out there.

So why is it that most Christians don't share the gospel? Why do we remain silent about the greatest thing that has ever happened to us? Why are we reticent about sharing the best piece of news other people will ever hear? At its most basic level, it's a matter of spiritual warfare. If we can be duped into believing that a comfortable and silent Christianity is okay, Satan wins the battle. He'd like nothing better than a mute church.

The following story may be fictitious, but I like it nonetheless. And it wouldn't surprise me if this had actually happened in some church at some point.

The setting is a business meeting in a church with congregational polity. You know the type. Members vote on all kinds of trivial matters but never talk about things that really matter.

In this particular church, the moderator of the meeting was a stickler for *Robert's Rules of Order*. No member ever challenged him because he had the most recent edition of *Robert's* memorized. The meeting had been contentious from the start, with a bitter debate over what color they should paint the fellowship hall.

When it came time for new business, an elderly gentleman asked to speak. He wanted to tell the congregation how he had shared the gospel with a teenager, and how that teenager had accepted Christ almost immediately. The church members were stunned into silence. Nothing like this had ever happened in one of their business meetings. Even the usually composed moderator was a bit flustered.

"We are all grateful to hear this story," he finally said with feigned sincerity. "But we are at 'new business' on the agenda, so I will have to rule you out of order."

The elderly gentleman stood and addressed the moderator and the other members at the meeting.

"Sir," he said softly but firmly, "if sharing the gospel is not the business of the church, then I suggest it's time for this church to go out of business."

The thesis of this book is simple: We must all learn to

share the gospel with ease. But this isn't so much a how-to book on evangelism as it is a reminder that God has given us all we need to share the Good News about his Son, Jesus Christ.

Do we fail to share the gospel because we're afraid we lack the ability? Do we fail to share the gospel because we think it's someone else's responsibility? A good friend told me recently that he is hesitant to share the gospel because he isn't sure what to say. We will address that subject in a subsequent chapter.

Based on surveys we've taken, our best estimate is that fewer than one in twenty Christians have ever had a gospel conversation with someone. Some may have had a few such conversations, but they don't have a *lifestyle* of sharing the gospel. And very few, it seems, are able to share the gospel with ease.

It's time to get rid of our excuses and make evangelism one of the highest priorities in our lives and our churches. Let's not forget: When we evangelize, we do so in God's power. If he is our power, we cannot fail.

GOD'S GOT THIS

I love watching my three sons in their roles as dads. They are amazing fathers, so much better than I ever was. I love watching my grandchildren run to their dads when they are afraid or have a perceived need. And I love watching my sons take care of them, protect them, and provide for them.

One evening, during a loud thunderstorm, my youngest son, Jess, embraced one of his children who had run to him in fear. He simply picked her up, held her tight, and whispered, "I've got you. It's okay, I've got you."

If only we would run into the embrace of our heavenly Father—with all the protection, power, and love he offers—we would never stumble in evangelism. We would never be fearful. We would share the gospel with ease.

Remember the promises we noted earlier in the two Great Commission passages:

> Be sure of this: I am with you always, even to the end of the age.
> MATTHEW 28:20

> You will receive power when the Holy Spirit comes upon you.
> ACTS 1:8

We are never commanded to share the gospel in our own strength or our own power. To the contrary, God always promises his power, his strength, and his presence.

Several years ago, we introduced a resource at Church Answers called Pray & Go (PrayAndGoChurch.com). The concept is simple. Two church members walk together through a neighborhood and pray for each home they pass. They don't make direct contact with anyone, but they leave a door hanger letting the residents know that someone has prayed for them. The door hanger has the church's address along with a phone number and email address for texting or emailing prayer requests. That's it.

We have been blown away by the responses from churches. Their members aren't knocking on doors or presenting the gospel to anyone directly. They are simply praying for the residents of each home. But the results have been encouraging.

Here's what one pastor said when some of his members used Pray & Go in their community.

"We had a goal to pray for two thousand homes in three months," he began. "We surpassed that number by more than a thousand homes. The church members really caught the vision."

Even the pastor was surprised with the evangelistic fruit of these efforts.

"We had so many members tell us about unexpected encounters with unbelievers," he said. "People would come up to them and ask them what they were doing. Many times people would get saved in a conversation on the sidewalk. It was incredible."

The pastor estimated that about twenty people have

become followers of Christ through this low-pressure, non-confrontational approach. He anticipates there will be many more, based on the number of homes where the members prayed.

"I get a lot of people wanting to know what our 'secret' is," he chuckled. "I tell them to simply get their people *praying* and *going*. It's a powerful combination that God honors. Our church members have learned that prayer-filled going gives them the opportunity to share the gospel with ease. They depend on God; they don't depend on themselves."

We will look more closely in another chapter at the power of prayer and evangelism. But for now, be encouraged by this simple assurance: God's got this.

COMMITTING TO BE A BEARER OF THE MOST IMPORTANT MESSAGE

God put this book in your hands for a reason. He wants it to remind you that you are responsible for conveying the most important message he has for the world. You are responsible for telling people the Good News of Jesus Christ. You are responsible for seeking God's power and strength through prayer.

I began this chapter by talking about Joe Hendrickson. When I became a believer, I didn't tell my parents at first. They didn't know that Coach Joe had witnessed to me. I'm not certain why I didn't share it with them, but I didn't.

Many years later, when I began writing books, I mentioned Coach Joe in the acknowledgments of one of my early publications, *The Book of Church Growth*:

> One final word. Some twenty-five years ago in Union Springs, Alabama, a high school football coach named Joe Hendrickson introduced me to the Savior whose church I write about in this book. I never thanked my coach for the eternal difference he made in my life, and I do not know where he is today. Perhaps somehow these words will find you, coach. Thank you for caring enough about one hungry little kid to tell him about the Bread of Life.[1]

I sent a copy of the book to my mom. When she received it in the mail, she called me and she was crying. She told me she had never heard the story about Coach Joe, and she was so ashamed that she had not shared the gospel with me when I was growing up. Of course she had been a strong influence in my life and a model of right living, and I told her as much, but she kept rebuking herself for not explicitly telling me the Good News of Jesus Christ. She would mention that big regret until the day she died.

Eventually, years later, I was reconnected with Coach Joe. I had written about him so much that one of his neighbors, who had read my books, let him know I was looking for him. He called the office at the organization I led at the time. Despite my precision in details, he wasn't certain the story was about him. He didn't remember the specific conversation with me.

When I heard his voice on the phone after so many years, I choked up. He did as well. Soon I was able to bring him to my company's headquarters, and we honored him and his family. He deserved that honor and so much more.

Coach Joe was God's instrument to introduce me to the Savior who would give me eternal life. He didn't just make all the difference in the world to me. He made all the difference in eternity.

Before you turn another page, before you read another word, will you commit to becoming a gospel bearer? Don't worry about the details. Don't worry about how doors will open. Just make a commitment to share the most important message ever.

It will make all the difference in the world . . . and eternity.

2

WHY WE ARE UNEASY

I have vivid memories of the first time I shared the gospel. I was twentysomething and had never uttered a word to an unbeliever about Jesus.

Then I met Jim.

Jim was in my small group. I'm not sure how he found out about us; he seemed to just show up one day. It didn't take long to find out Jim's story. His wife had recently left him for a coworker. He hadn't seen it coming, and he was devastated.

He had never been to church, but felt that he needed to start going. Though quiet and shy by nature, Jim readily told me about his loneliness and pain. He was hoping he could find something at our church to fill the void in his life.

I knew beyond a shadow of a doubt that someone needed to tell Jim about Jesus. He was not a Christian, but he was seeking.

Then it hit me. *I* needed to tell him about Jesus.

The very thought of talking to an unbeliever about Jesus made my heart race so fast that I felt like I was close to hyperventilating. I rationalized that someone else could do it. I thought that if Jim came to church often enough, he would hear the gospel. I could just wait for the process to unfold.

But God did not let me wait. He wanted me to tell Jim about Jesus.

I went to my pastor and shared my perceived dilemma. He gave me a book about sharing the gospel. It required me to memorize a lot of words. I wasn't ready for that. I just needed to have a conversation with Jim.

I mustered my courage and asked Jim if I could drop by his apartment that night. Much to my chagrin, he said he would love for me to visit.

I wish you could have seen me that day. No, I take that back. I am glad you didn't see me that day. I was a nervous wreck. Not only was my heart beating double time, but my hands were clammy and my throat was dry and tight. I don't think I prayed as much for Jim's salvation that day as I did for my own survival.

When I entered Jim's apartment, he could tell I was really nervous. He felt comfortable enough to ask me what my problem was. The words that came out of my mouth were certainly not what I had planned.

"Jim, you don't want to go to hell, do you?"

Good grief. I knew I had messed up, and I could feel my face turn red.

Then Jim spoke.

"No, I don't, Thom," he said softly. "Can you tell me how to go to heaven?"

I can only imagine that my expression was one of total perplexity. Had Jim really opened the door that wide?

Indeed he had, and he became my brother in Christ that evening. I left his apartment amazed at how everything had transpired. I left with joy because Jim had accepted Christ. And I left with thanksgiving because God had given me everything I needed for that encounter.

THE BATTLE

I get it. I understand why so many people do not share the gospel with others. I've been there and done that. Indeed, I still have lapses today.

The ultimate issue goes back to our discussion in the previous chapter. Satan does not want us to share the gospel. He will do everything he can to stop us. Evangelism is a major threat to him. He wants the souls of men and women to populate hell.

I'm convinced the devil will attack us at our greatest points of vulnerability to keep us silent. And we may not even realize it's happening.

I am a classic introvert, quiet and shy by nature. I prefer that others speak while I listen. Many people who have only seen me in public or heard me on podcasts or webinars are surprised. I can appear to be outgoing, but it goes against my natural personality.

On many occasions, my introversion has stopped me from sharing the gospel. Let me rephrase that: On many occasions, I have used my quiet and shy nature as a convenient excuse not to share the gospel. I succumb to the wiles of the devil rather than demonstrate obedience to God.

Satan will exploit our weaknesses to render us silent. But our natural inclinations and abilities are no excuse for silence. We must trust in the power of God to overcome our inadequacies. When we do, we gain victory in the spiritual battle for the souls of men and women. God's grace is more than sufficient. And his power works best in our weakness (see 2 Corinthians 12:9).

WHEN WE DO NOT PRACTICE THE DISCIPLINES

A spiritual discipline is a habit we develop in God's power to become more like Jesus. When we practice the spiritual discipline of reading God's Word, we grow as Christians.

When we practice the spiritual disciplines of prayer and fasting, we mature in our faith. When we practice the spiritual discipline of gathering with fellow believers in our churches, we are being obedient to Christ.

All these disciplines help us become better at what we do. Specifically, they help us become more like Christ, who strengthens us to be obedient to him.

Evangelism is a spiritual discipline. So how do we become more effective at this discipline? In God's power, we become better at what we do when we do it more regularly.

Athletes don't become good at what they do unless they practice regularly. Outstanding physicians are at their best when they refine their skills through repetition. Writers become better writers when they write.

You get the point. Many Christians do not share the gospel *with ease* because they do not share the gospel *regularly*.

The most effective gospel sharers I have known maintain a discipline of sharing their faith regularly. They practice their proclamation. You won't become more effective at evangelism until you actually start evangelizing. It's such a commonsense issue, but many of us get out of the habit—or never get into it in the first place. Our discipline becomes lax. And thus, our witness becomes less effective.

One of my mentors, the late Lewis Drummond, was a professor of mine at seminary. He loved to tell stories about one of his friends, Mr. M. L. O'Neal—though Dr. Drummond always called him by his last name. O'Neal, he told us, could not help but share his faith. He seemed to be like Peter and John—who, when told to stop talking about Jesus lest they face further imprisonment and even death, said, "We cannot stop telling about everything we have seen and heard" (Acts 4:20).

Week after week in class, we would hear stories about O'Neal. Even when Dr. Drummond repeated one of his favorites, we listened with fascination and amusement. We loved hearing how O'Neal would find himself in all types of predicaments but would somehow find a way to share the gospel.

One day when I was driving Dr. Drummond to the airport, I asked him about O'Neal. What made him so effective at sharing the gospel? How was he so continuously bold with others?

"Well, friend," Dr. Drummond began as he often did, "if you had known O'Neal when he was younger, you would never have expected him to become such a bold witness for Jesus. But O'Neal became convicted that he was supposed to share his faith. He saw that the Bible said he must be a gospel bearer."

I didn't sense that Dr. Drummond was getting to the essence of my question, so I asked again.

"But how did he become so effective?"

Dr. Drummond smiled. "I wouldn't call him effective in his early years. But I would call him persistent. He just kept sharing his faith, even with nervousness and uncertainty. I guess the more he practiced evangelism, the more effective he became. I can't explain it any other way."

Evangelism is a discipline. The more you do it, the better you will become.

Let me qualify that. The more you practice evangelism *in God's power*, the better you will become.

Many Christians are uneasy with evangelism because they don't approach it in a disciplined way. It's really that basic. The more you share the gospel, the more comfortable you will become.

DO YOU REALLY BELIEVE?

By all external measures, Mike was a good church member. He hardly missed a worship service. He was in our community group and attended every week. At the time I spoke with him, he had served on his church's welcome team for three years. I was dean of a seminary and was serving the church as an interim pastor. That meant I preached every Sunday and met with the staff once a week.

I was preaching through the book of Acts, and because Acts has so many clear examples of sharing the gospel, I was able to bring up the topic of personal evangelism on several occasions. I guess it became my theme as I covered the book chapter by chapter.

It was in that context that Mike asked to meet with me.

I looked forward to our meal together. Mike was a positive guy. He seemed really good for the church, and he was a vocal supporter of mine. I never would have expected the conversation we were about to have.

I could tell something was different about Mike as soon as we sat down at the restaurant. He wasn't his usual jovial self. He seemed subdued and introspective. Though I don't remember the conversation with precision, it went something like this.

"So, what's up, Mike?"

Stirring his salad nervously with his fork, Mike replied, "I'm struggling with your sermons, Thom."

Here we go, I thought. Mike wasn't the first person—nor would he be the last—to have a problem with my preaching. But I never expected *him* to be one of my critics.

"Tell me your problem," I responded. I wasn't sure I really wanted to hear it, but I had to ask.

Mike paused carefully and thoughtfully before beginning to speak.

"You're talking a lot about evangelism," he said.

I nodded.

"In fact, you are talking a lot about our responsibility to share the gospel."

Again, I nodded. Then he dropped the bomb.

"Thom," he said with some difficulty, "I don't think I can do personal evangelism, because I don't believe in it."

He knew I was stunned and waiting for his next sentence.

"How can I feel an urgency to tell people about Christ if I have my own doubts that he is the only way of salvation?"

Wow. This lunch was not going as planned.

I tried to maintain some semblance of composure, but I wasn't doing a very good job. He had hit a nerve.

"Mike," I said with measured intensity, "Jesus himself said he was the only way of salvation."

Mike looked at me blankly.

"Remember how Jesus says in John 14:6, 'I am the way, the truth, and the life. No one can come to the Father except through me'? Mike, either Jesus is who he says he is, or he's a liar or a lunatic." I was paraphrasing an argument put forth by C. S. Lewis in *Mere Christianity*.[2]

Again, Mike just looked at me. He knew the biblical argument. He just didn't believe it.

I knew I was crossing a line when I questioned Mike's salvation. But how can we really say we have accepted Jesus if we don't accept who he says he is?

Mike did not flinch. He was smart. He was already asking himself that same question.

Though the conversation was grueling, it was indeed enlightening. So much of our contemporary culture wants to think of Jesus as a good man or a noble prophet. But they don't want to accept him as the Lord of creation and the only way of salvation.

The precise name of this doctrine that offends people is *exclusivity*. It is the belief that Jesus is not *a* way of salvation; he is *the* way of salvation.

Exclusivity is hard for our culture to accept. People may be willing to concede that Jesus has a special role in history. But they're not willing to accept that there is no other way to heaven. From their perspective, exclusivity is a narrow-minded and prejudicial posture.

But without Jesus, there is no death on the cross. Without his death on the cross and shed blood, there is no forgiveness of sins. Without forgiveness of sins, we cannot enter heaven.

With Jesus, on the other hand, we can be confident of these things:

No one else died for our sins.

No one else was fully God and fully man.

No one else can get us to heaven in right standing before God the Father.

No one else is the way of salvation.

Though I disagreed fervently with Mike's conclusion, I could understand his perspective. If Jesus is not the only way of salvation, if there are multiple ways to heaven, or if everyone goes to heaven, why should I feel any urgency to tell others about Jesus?

Many church leaders might be surprised to find out how many of their members really doubt the doctrine of exclusivity. Some might be pluralists, holding the belief that there are many ways to heaven other than through Jesus. Some might be inclusivists, believing that Jesus can be found in other religions. Still others might be universalists. They believe everyone goes to heaven.

Then there is a growing belief in annihilationism. Those who are not believers do not go to an eternal hell; they simply cease to exist.

Any one of these beliefs would take away our motivation for evangelism. Why should we plead with others to accept Jesus if he is really not the only way of salvation?

Simply stated, bad theology kills evangelism.

IT'S SOMEONE ELSE'S RESPONSIBILITY

Nellie Jo and I recently kept five of our grandchildren for the weekend. One of the younger ones, who will remain unnamed, has a propensity to turn upside down any room he goes into. Rugs are moved. Chairs stacked on top of each other. Sofa cushions scattered on the floor as make-believe rocks on quicksand. For some reason, this time the television screen was facing the wall.

I had gently reminded this grandchild not to destroy the room as he had done previously. So when I walked into the room and saw the latest disaster he had wrought, he knew he was in trouble. He was caught red-handed. Alone. None of the other grandkids was even on the same floor.

When I asked him how the chaos had unfolded, he deflected the responsibility to his sister. "She did it," he said with remarkable certainty and conviction. When I reminded him that his sister wasn't even home at the moment, he quickly shifted gears.

"Well," he said, "it's a miracle."

Nope. There was no miracle. As much as my grandson tried to avoid accountability, he alone was responsible for the mess.

Christians can be quick to deflect responsibility, especially when it comes to evangelism. As the new pastor in my second church, I decided to have a question-and-answer time for a few minutes after the worship service. When someone asked me about my vision for the future of the church, I began to gush about seeing dozens of church members eventually sharing their faith.

I was quickly interrupted by one of the older ladies in the church.

"You can forget that, Pastor," she said indignantly. "That's what we pay *you* to do."

That was the only time I've ever heard a church member say those words out loud. But I know that many Christians have a "hired hand" view of evangelism. They don't share the gospel because that's what they pay the pastor and staff to do. They couldn't imagine doing otherwise.

Another convenient deflection is often articulated like

this: "It's not my spiritual gift." Though some scholars debate whether evangelism is a spiritual gift or an office of church leadership, let's assume for argument's sake that it's a spiritual gift. This would mean that some gifted believers are better able to articulate the gospel, and perhaps will see more people become followers of Christ. But does it mean that other Christians are thus excused from the Great Commission mandate? Absolutely not!

I don't have the spiritual gift of mercy. Does that mean I am excused from showing mercy to others? Again, the question is rhetorical. Though spiritual gifts may point Christians toward specific areas of service, no one is excused from demonstrating the qualities of Christian character, even in areas where they may not be particularly gifted.

The Great Commission is a general commandment to all believers. Jesus didn't select only certain Christians with specific gifts or callings to share the gospel. He gave the mandate to all believers—from the first century to the twenty-first century and beyond.

As described in Acts 1:8, believers were to share the gospel "in Jerusalem, throughout Judea, in Samaria, and to the ends of the earth." The message is clear: Share the gospel first where you are, then be willing to take it to places beyond your immediate context.

Though Luke wrote the book of Acts with great precision, he doesn't tell us *why* the believers stayed in Jerusalem, even though they had clearly been commanded to share the gospel beyond the boundaries of the city where the first church was started. It's hard to fathom that it was because they were too comfortable. Many had left their families to follow Jesus. And it seems unlikely these early believers grew complacent that quickly.

Perhaps they were simply adjusting to the new reality of the church as the living body of Christ. Perhaps they were still trying to figure out how to move forward without the incarnate presence of Jesus with them. But they apparently stayed in Jerusalem even though God was ready for them to move outward.

It took persecution to get them moving, as we see in Acts 8:1: "A great wave of persecution began that day, sweeping over the church in Jerusalem; and all the believers except the apostles were scattered through the regions of Judea and Samaria."

Well, persecution is one way to motivate people to action.

It's also interesting to note that all the believers *except the apostles* began to scatter. So much for hanging the mantle of responsibility on leadership. Did God assign an elite group of early church members to share the gospel? Did he ask for a show of hands from everyone who had the gift of evangelism? No.

Acts 8:4 gives us a clear picture of those who were commissioned to do the work of evangelism: "The believers who were scattered preached the Good News about Jesus wherever they went." Simply stated, *everyone* shared the gospel. Not only the gifted. Not only the leaders. Not only those who had social status. *Everyone*.

So yes, it's someone else's responsibility. And if you're a Christian, you are among the "someone else."

FOR THE BUSY AMONG US

When the COVID pandemic came crashing into the world in 2020, I devoured any information I could find about it. I wanted to be able to help churches and church leaders during that tumultuous time. I pointed them to digital worship for a season. I helped them move their giving to online platforms. I wanted them to be prepared to regather when the time came.[3]

I'll admit I had one clear expectation for the time of quarantine during the pandemic. I expected everyone to slow down and get their priorities in order.

By and large, that did not happen.

There were exceptions, of course. I've heard some couples say that the downtime was a healthy interlude for their marriage. Some people read books they had been meaning to get to. Many Christians used the pause to pray and read their Bibles more.

But most people, it seems, Christians included, became busier.

Many parents who transitioned to working from home also became de facto homeschool teachers. Workers found themselves spending more time in meetings—on Zoom, Teams, or some other platform. Many pastors saw their sermon prep time curtailed by the need to record an online or streaming message ahead of time while trying to take care of the evolving needs of their church members. On top of all that were new conversations, decisions, criticisms, and divided opinions about wearing masks, social distancing, and whether and when to regather. Many church leaders indeed became busier.

Busyness is a common plight for most of us. And it is a common reason—or convenient excuse—for those who don't share the gospel on a regular basis. But it's not a valid excuse.

When we put the busyness of life before the priority of evangelism, we demonstrate what really matters to us—and what really doesn't matter. If we have time to follow our favorite sports teams, do we not have time to share the gospel? If we have time to look at Instagram, Facebook, YouTube, and other social media, do we not have time to share the gospel? And if we have time for all our devices, do we not have time to share the gospel?

The reality is that *no one* is really too busy. God has gifted everyone with the same 24 hours each day and 168 hours each week. He expects us to steward that precious gift of time faithfully. If we're too busy to share the gospel, we're too busy for God. Human nature says that we will ultimately do the things that are most important to us. If that doesn't include telling others about Jesus, we are essentially saying we don't care if people go to heaven or to hell.

Are you really too busy to share your faith?

BUT I WILL MAKE THEM UNCOMFORTABLE

Before I answered God's call to vocational ministry, I worked in the business world and did well. I was promoted quickly and received responsibilities for which I definitely was not prepared.

One of those moments was a heart-to-heart conversation with a man who reported directly to me. He was bright, but lacked a good work ethic. He took advantage of his perks and privileges, but didn't get his work done. It was my responsibility to get him moving in the right direction or ask him to leave.

I had never had one of those tough conversations with a worker, and I was nervous. At the age of twenty-six, I had little experience and certainly little wisdom. The CEO of our organization was wise and a bit salty. Finally I got up the nerve to ask him how he handled these types of conversations. In his own earthy way, he told me he had reached the point where he knew that being confronted was for the person's own good. I would be giving my direct report an opportunity to make needed and necessary changes.

The CEO also said that the organization as a whole would suffer if we did not provide proper direction and correction for the people under our leadership. He convinced me that the meeting was necessary for the good of everyone.

I was uncomfortable, but I moved forward. My direct report was even more uncomfortable when I confronted him. Sadly, though given every opportunity to make the necessary changes, he did not do so, and we soon let him go.

Telling people about Jesus might make them uncomfortable. But is it really that big an issue if they feel some discomfort? Is it not okay for people to be a bit uneasy if the Holy Spirit is at work in their lives? After all, you are presenting them with good news, an offer to receive the free gift of forgiveness and eternal life. Momentary discomfort is a small price to pay for an eternal offer.

But people are not always uneasy when we start gospel conversations. Some are even eager to hear what we have to say.

Avoiding discomfort is not really a good excuse when eternity is in the balance.

WE'RE NOT REALLY SURE WHAT TO SAY

If you ask a typical Christian how he or she became a Christian, a common response is, "I accepted Jesus Christ as my Lord and Savior." It's a good response. It's a response that summarizes their response to the gospel. The challenge is that many non-Christians don't know what it means to accept Jesus Christ as Lord and Savior. And for many non-Christians, the conversation becomes even murkier if you ask them if they want to accept Jesus into their hearts. What does it mean to accept Jesus into your heart?

When Christians use jargon, it creates a communication problem.

I saw a classic case of this miscommunication when I was a pastor in St. Petersburg, Florida, many years ago. A man who visited our church—I'll call him George—was obviously eager to learn more about spiritual matters.

He and I went to a local seafood restaurant so we could get to know each other better. In the course of the conversation, George told me he was a Christian. But so much of what he said indicated otherwise.

I asked him when he had become a Christian. He told me that while he was living in a different town, someone had come to his home and invited him to church. In the course of the conversation, the man from the church asked George if he was a Christian. When George replied in the negative, the man offered to show him how to become a follower of Christ.

Essentially, he led George in a prayer in which George articulated that he wanted to accept Jesus as his Lord and

Savior. The man then congratulated George and told him he was saved.

I inquired, "George, what did it mean to you when you prayed for Jesus to be your Lord and Savior?" He responded in words I recall to this day: "It meant I believed Jesus was one of the greatest men ever to live, and I should try to live like he did."

He knew nothing about repentance and faith.

He had never heard that Jesus was the only way of salvation.

He thought he had to work hard at being a Christian. He knew nothing about the free gift of salvation.

As we continued our conversation, it became quite apparent that George was not a Christian. But when I shared the gospel with him, he was ready to repent and place his faith in Jesus. Even though he had "accepted Jesus as his Lord and Savior," he knew something was missing. He had redefined those words well beyond their biblical meaning.

Let me be clear. God can and often does work in people's lives when we present a less-than-thorough gospel. I've seen the Holy Spirit take inadequate words and use them to convict people of their sin. But I have also seen a lot of people like George. We must make certain we communicate biblical truth in sharing the gospel with people.

In the next chapter, we will dive into the meaning of "the gospel." It doesn't require multiple theological degrees to share this eternal truth, but we must make sure we communicate the essence of the gospel. It's important.

THE BEHAVIOR OF CHRISTIANS EMBARRASSES ME

I was in a casual conversation with a fellow member of the church I attend. We both want to be more effective in our Christian witness, and he shared with me his biggest challenge. "Thom," he began, "I have tried starting conversations about my faith with coworkers. So many of them immediately point to the misbehavior of other Christians as a reason why they don't want to be a Christian. They either point out a Christian leader who has messed up, or they refer to social media postings of some Christians."

My friend is rather blunt, so his next sentence did not surprise me. "Some Christians are just stupid on social media, especially if they get into political arguments."

The problem isn't new. Though we've been forgiven, no Christian is perfect. But we can't let the sins of other believers stop us from telling people how their sins can be forgiven. In fact, this so-called excuse can be an opportunity to point out grace and forgiveness. While acknowledging the imperfections of all Christians, including ourselves, we still must show them Jesus.

Our own sinfulness can often hinder us from sharing our faith. The enemy loves for us to think we're not good enough to tell others about Jesus. The evil one desires our silence, and he will remind us of all our sins, even those in the distant past.

I served as a bi-vocational pastor in my first church. I could not support my family on my church salary of fifty dollars a week, so I kept my job as a banker, as well.

I had so many good opportunities to share the gospel at that bank. It was a reminder of the incredible opportunities we have in the marketplace. God blessed me as some of my coworkers became followers of Christ. On one occasion, though, I really blew it. I lost my temper when a coworker told me I had to get something done by the end of the day. And I did not do a good job of hiding my anger in front of others.

I could use the excuse that I was tired from my work as a pastor, banker, and seminary student, but that's really not a good excuse.

When I returned to the bank the next day, I apologized to those who had seen me lose my cool. I admitted to them how wrong I was. I let them know that, even as a Christian, I still mess up.

My coworkers showed an amazing level of understanding. They accepted my apologies. They kept the door open for me to continue to share Christ with them.

God still used me, a really messed-up sinner. And God can still use you, even when you blow it and embarrass the faith.

That is the power of the gospel—the subject of our next chapter.

3

UNDERSTANDING
THE GOSPEL

I have a strange nightmare several times a year. I'm about to take an exam in college, but I have not prepared for it at all. I'm dreading the moment. My heart is racing, and my breathing is labored. I know I will fail and my life will come crashing down around me.

There must be some basic psychological explanation behind this recurring dream. Frankly, I've never pursued any analysis. I'm sure there are worse nightmares to have, and life goes on when I wake up.

On the other hand, I've had some real-life moments when I should have been better prepared but wasn't. Those are no fun at all.

One area where a lack of preparation can have eternal

significance in someone's life is our own understanding of the gospel. We may hesitate to share our faith because we're afraid we can't answer people's questions or deal with their objections.

To be effective witnesses for Christ, we must be prepared both spiritually and mentally. In this chapter, we will look at the essence of the gospel. Volumes have been written on the subject, so the brief synopsis here is only a starting point. On the other hand, you may only have time to present a brief synopsis during a conversation, so it's a good starting point.

The main thing is to be prepared. Perhaps someone notices something different about you. Though you haven't explicitly spoken about your faith, they see it coming through in your life. Maybe they ask you a question. They want to know why you are different or why you behave the way you do. As the apostle Peter reminds us, "If someone asks you about your hope as a believer, always be ready to explain it" (1 Peter 3:15).

The place to begin is with the nature of God himself.

"IN THE BEGINNING, GOD . . ."

Theology books are filled with descriptions of the nature and character of God. He is omnipotent, the all-powerful God. He is omniscient, the all-knowing God. He is omnipresent, the God who is not limited by time and space.

Perhaps the best place to begin is by understanding God as a *creator*. After all, that's where the Bible begins.

The book of Genesis opens with this incredible verse: "In the beginning God created the heavens and the earth." The creation account continues with God's forming of all creatures, culminating with his greatest creation: *human beings*.

> Then God said, "Let us make human beings in our image, to be like us. They will reign over the fish in the sea, the birds in the sky, the livestock, all the wild animals on the earth, and the small animals that scurry along the ground." So God created human beings in his own image. In the image of God he created them; male and female he created them.
>
> GENESIS 1:26-27

We are all God's creation. Without him willing us to exist by the power of his word, there would be no earth, no animals, no planets and stars, and—most important—no humans.

A proper understanding of God must grasp the truth that we, and everything that exists, were created by him and are under his dominion. We are not the result of random chance; we were created by the one true and living God. God gives us the hope of the gospel because he desires to redeem that which he created.

Because we were created by God, we are under his total authority. He has every right to tell his creation how to live. God is not arbitrary. He knows what is best for us. We often act as if we know better than God how we should live and what we should do.

The apostle Paul sums up this argument well: "Who are you, a mere human being, to argue with God? Should the thing that was created say to the one who created it, 'Why have you made me like this?' When a potter makes jars out of clay, doesn't he have a right to use the same lump of clay to make one jar for decoration and another to throw garbage into?" (Romans 9:20-21).

We must also grasp that God is perfect and holy and righteous. The psalmist declares: "The LORD is king! Let the earth rejoice! Let the farthest coastlands be glad. Dark clouds surround him. Righteousness and justice are the foundations of his throne" (Psalm 97:1-2).

What, then, is the foundation of God's kingship? It is *righteousness* and *justice*. When God revealed himself to Moses, he began by calling out his own name and his own attributes:

Yahweh! The LORD! The God of compassion and mercy! I am slow to anger and filled with unfailing

love and faithfulness. I lavish unfailing love to a
thousand generations. I forgive iniquity, rebellion,
and sin. But I do not excuse the guilty.
EXODUS 34:6-7

We take great comfort in God calling himself compassionate and merciful. We rejoice in his unfailing love and faithfulness. We are moved that he forgives iniquity, rebellion, and sin.

But don't stop reading there. Look at the last sentence: "But I do not excuse the guilty."

God is indeed loving. God is indeed faithful. God indeed forgives rebellion and sin. But God is also righteous and just: He does not excuse the guilty. A truly righteous and holy God cannot overlook or ignore sin. The God of truth and justice must deal with sin. This means that everyone who is a sinner must face the justice of God. Including you and me.

FOR ALL HAVE SINNED . . .

Romans 3:23 is probably in the top ten of most-memorized Bible verses: "Everyone has sinned; we all fall short of God's glorious standard." This is Paul's powerful reminder to us that we are *all* sinners; *no one* even comes close to the glory of God.

Have you ever broken a law? Perhaps your response is like mine: "More times than I care to admit."

Let me give you one example.

Recently, I purchased a car. When I called my insurance agent to transfer coverage, he asked me a question I hadn't heard before: "Are you interested in saving some money on your premium by having a monitor on your vehicle?"

Perhaps you're familiar with automobile monitors. They track your speed, the speed limit, and your braking. In other words, with a monitor on your vehicle, your insurance company will know if you are speeding or driving recklessly. Drivers who obey the letter of the law can qualify for lower insurance rates.

You probably can guess how I replied.

No, thanks.

I don't consider myself a reckless driver, but I'm not comfortable with my insurance company knowing where I am and how fast I got there. I've read articles by privacy experts who caution against giving out too much personal information.

But let's be honest. I give my credit card number countless places. Amazon probably knows as much about me as I do myself. My smartphone company can tell you all sorts of things about me: where I travel; what I eat; where I make purchases; what I read. The list goes on. I have not turned in my smartphone for privacy concerns. I have not canceled my Amazon account for privacy concerns. And I still post on some social media sites.

Simply stated, I didn't want the car monitor because I know I drive five or six miles per hour over the limit on occasion and I don't want to get caught speeding by my insurance company. Though it's hard for me to write these words, I forfeited a decent savings on my insurance premium because I anticipate breaking the law.

Of course, it's easy to rationalize it. I'm really not hurting anyone. I'm not being dangerous. And some speed limits are ridiculously slow, like the 17 mph limit in my neighborhood. But those are just excuses. I'm still breaking the law. You might even say I'm *planning* to break the law.

We can look at sin with that same lens. "I'm not really hurting anyone with my 'small' sins." "I told that lie because I didn't want to hurt her feelings." "I just borrowed that item. I'll return it later."

But sin is not a simple infraction like driving a few miles over the speed limit. Sin breaks our relationship with our holy and perfect God. In essence, when we sin we're telling God we will not obey him; we will not submit to his authority. When we sin, we're rebelling against our perfect God.

When God created humanity, he desired and planned for us to be in perfect fellowship with him, worshiping him and rejoicing in him. God created us in his image and placed all of creation under our authority:

God created human beings in his own image.
In the image of God he created them; male and
female he created them. Then God blessed them
and said, "Be fruitful and multiply. Fill the earth
and govern it. Reign over the fish in the sea, the
birds in the sky, and all the animals that scurry
along the ground."

GENESIS 1:27-28

We were meant to govern the earth and reign over creation. God put humanity in charge of all creation—with one important caveat. We were still under God's ultimate authority.

You know the story. God gives Adam and Eve free rein over the Garden, with one exception. God tells Adam, "You may freely eat the fruit of every tree in the garden—except the tree of the knowledge of good and evil. If you eat its fruit, you are sure to die" (Genesis 2:16-17).

Then the devil comes in the form of a serpent and contradicts God's warning about the forbidden fruit.

"You won't die!" the serpent replied to the woman.
"God knows that your eyes will be opened as soon as
you eat it, and you will be like God, knowing both
good and evil."

GENESIS 3:4-5

So Eve falls to temptation, Adam falls along with her, and sin enters the world.

We mustn't see the Fall as merely a failure to obey a trivial and arbitrary rule. No, God had every right and all authority to tell Adam and Eve what to do and what not to do. They were subject to him, and they chose to disobey him. They rebelled against their creator. They chose to sin. "So the LORD God banished them from the Garden of Eden" (Genesis 3:23).

We can point fingers at Adam and Eve all we want, but the Bible makes it clear that the first humans are not the only ones guilty of sin. Read these powerful words from Romans 3:10-18:

> No one is righteous—not even one. No one is truly wise; no one is seeking God. All have turned away; all have become useless. No one does good, not a single one. Their talk is foul, like the stench from an open grave. Their tongues are filled with lies. Snake venom drips from their lips. Their mouths are full of cursing and bitterness. They rush to commit murder. Destruction and misery always follow them. They don't know where to find peace. They have no fear of God at all.

It is powerful and clear. We all have sinned. We all have fallen short of God's glory. But God sent his one and only Son to rescue and redeem us.

His name is Jesus.

JESUS IS THE SAVIOR

My dad was a top turret gunner on a B-24 Liberator in World War II. Though I don't know the precise fatality rate of those who flew those dangerous missions, I do know many airmen were killed in action. Dad told me he flew far more missions than he originally expected, and the survival rate for so many missions was very low.

Though his plane was severely damaged on several occasions, he and his crew returned from every mission. Dad was badly wounded by shrapnel and was awarded the Purple Heart. But he survived.

But I didn't know the rest of the story until I went to sit with my dad as he lay dying from an aggressive cancer at sixty-two years of age.

I had only one question that day. Other conversations could wait, if we had any more days left together. But I wanted to know my father's salvation story. I wanted to be certain he was going to heaven. I wanted to make sure he had that assurance as well.

His story centered on the days of World War II. He

had completely yielded both his physical and eternal life to Christ before he left for England to fly those missions over Germany. And he had promised God that if he returned from World War II, he would marry Nan, my mother. He did not want to marry her before he left because he did not want her to become a widow.

He wanted me to understand that it was a *promise*, not a deal with God—not something he would do if God held up his end of the bargain and let him survive. It was simply a promise to God to fulfill a vow.

I told him how proud I was of him, and I told him it was truly a romantic story.

My dad then looked me straight in the eye and said, "Son, that's not the full story. I also told God that if he blessed us with children, I would dedicate them to the service of the Lord. I should have told you that story before now, but you need to know. Thom, you are the fulfillment of a promise I made to God."

I was stunned. I was emotional. I was in mild shock.

You are the fulfillment of a promise I made to God.

In the months after Dad's death, I began to think of a multitude of *what-ifs*. What if Dad had died in World War II? What if he'd changed his mind about marrying my mom? What if she had decided not to wait for him?

All of those questions were moot because my dad survived

the war. He married my mother. I was born. And I have sought to serve the Lord most of my life.

But it's a worthwhile question: *What if?*

What if we had to pay the price for our sins? What if God had not become human and dwelt among us? What if Jesus had not died on the cross to save us?

The Good News, the gospel, is that we don't have to dwell on what-ifs. Jesus is God in the flesh: "The Word became human and made his home among us. He was full of unfailing love and faithfulness. And we have seen his glory, the glory of the Father's one and only son" (John 1:14). Jesus is fully God and fully human.

Jesus' mission was clear. It was announced by the angel to Joseph when Mary was found to be pregnant with Jesus.

> She will have a son, and you are to name him Jesus, for he will save his people from their sins.
>
> MATTHEW 1:21

What if?

What if Christ had not gone to the cross? What if he had not willingly chosen to die for us? What if he had decided he didn't want to pay a ransom to rescue us from sin and the devil?

The Good News, the gospel, is that—once again—all of those what-ifs are moot. Jesus did go to the cross. He took our sins upon himself.

> God made Christ, who never sinned, to be the
> offering for our sin, so that we could be made right
> with God through Christ.
>
> 2 CORINTHIANS 5:21

Like the lambs that were sacrificed by the priests in the Old Testament, Jesus, the perfect Lamb of God, became the sacrifice for our sins. When the sin of the world was cast upon him, his own Father could not look at him.

God turned away. Darkness fell on the land.

> At about three o'clock, Jesus called out with a loud
> voice, *"Eli, Eli, lema sabachthani?"* which means "My
> God, my God, why have you abandoned me?"
>
> MATTHEW 27:46

He who had never sinned became sin for me. For you. For the world.

We don't have to ask, "What if?" All of the answers have been given in Jesus. He is our Savior.

But we know the story did not end on the cross. Jesus died on the cross. His body was taken and placed securely in a borrowed tomb. A rock was rolled across the doorway to secure the tomb. And then, on the third day, Jesus rose from the dead. He not only defeated sin; he also defeated death.

Then the angel spoke to the women [who had come to the tomb]. "Don't be afraid!" he said. "I know you are looking for Jesus, who was crucified. He isn't here! He is risen from the dead, just as he said would happen. Come, see where his body was lying."

MATTHEW 28:5-6

That's the gospel, the Good News. Jesus died for our sins.

That's the gospel, the Good News. Jesus rose from the dead.

That's the gospel, the Good News. Because he lives, so can we.

OUR RESPONSE: REPENTANCE AND FAITH

Again and again, John the Baptist reminded the people who came to hear him preach that someone was coming who was much greater than he. Waiting with anticipation for the arrival of Jesus, John baptized many as he proclaimed the coming Messiah.

John would later have the tremendous privilege of baptizing the Savior of whom he had spoken. After the baptism, Jesus went into the wilderness for forty days where he was tempted by Satan and protected by angels.

It was time for Jesus to begin his mission on earth. So he went to Galilee and preached a message succinctly recorded in the Gospel of Mark: "The time promised by God has come at last! . . . The Kingdom of God is near! Repent of your sins and believe the Good News!" (Mark 1:15).

Repent and believe. The message is simple in its brevity and profound in its deep significance. We must repent—that is, we must turn away from sin. Repentance is not merely an apology for our sin. It's not one of those non-apologies we hear far too often: "I would like to apologize to anyone I may have offended." When I hear such "apologies," I cringe. Where is the repentance in those words?

No, repentance is far more than simply an apology. Though a sincere apology asks forgiveness for a single deed, repentance involves *action*—turning away from sin and moving in a different direction. And there is no "anyone I may have offended" in repentance. Repentance recognizes that our sin is an affront to our holy God.

When Paul appeared before King Agrippa, he clearly defined the meaning of repentance: "All must repent of their sins and turn to God—and prove they have changed by the good things they do" (Acts 26:20).

In the same breath, Paul declares both *repentance* (turning away from sin) and *faith* (turning to God). He then explains that true repentance will result in a changed life. In other words, you were walking away from God, but you did an about-face and now you are moving toward God. And your actions *prove* the reality of your repentance.

I have heard many testimonies from Christians who said they "accepted Jesus" as their Savior, at some point in their life, and became a Christian. But later they accepted Jesus as *Lord*.

But it doesn't work that way. We cannot separate Jesus as Savior from Jesus as Lord. If we truly believe by faith that Jesus is the Savior of the world and of our lives, we must also repent—turning away from our sin—and submit ourselves to Jesus as our Lord. Becoming a Christian is not a two-step process. Repentance and faith go hand in hand.

Faith, too, requires *action* that goes beyond mere belief. Yes, it includes believing that Jesus died for your sins, that he rose from the dead, and that he will forgive you and give you eternal life. But faith also means *trusting* what Christ has done, which is rooted in both history and eternity. Though we don't see Jesus visibly today, we trust unwaveringly that he is God, that he came as a man and lived among us, and that he will return for us someday. The writer of Hebrews says it powerfully: "Faith shows the reality of what we hope for; it is the evidence of things we cannot see" (Hebrews 11:1).

One day we will stand before God at the judgment seat of Christ. What will our plea be as to why God should allow us into his presence? As Christians we know we have done nothing to earn our salvation. We know that apart from Christ we have no righteousness at all. And we know we responded to the gospel by faith alone. We repented of our sins. And we were made right by the blood of Christ, which was shed on our behalf on the cross.

This is the message we must convey to those who are not yet Christians. We don't have to recite an expansive theological treatise, but we must communicate the essence and truth of the gospel.

Evangelism without the truth of the gospel is not evangelism at all.

THE POWER OF THE GOSPEL

We cannot understand the gospel fully unless we understand its power. The gospel is powerful because its message radically transforms people's lives. The gospel is transformative in every aspect of our lives. Those who have accepted the truth of the gospel have left the kingdom of darkness and entered the Kingdom of light. We have a new birth in Christ, and we are citizens of a new land.

The gospel message carries with it the power of Christ. The first time I shared the gospel, I was anything but eloquent. I'm certain I left out parts of the gospel message that should have been included. But Jim was nonetheless convicted by the Holy Spirit. He repented of his sins and placed his faith in Christ. Despite my verbal and emotional inadequacies, Jim still became a Christian.

We must understand that the power is not our own. It belongs wholly to God.

Keep in mind the *complete* Great Commission laid out in Matthew 28—beginning with verse 18: "Jesus came and told his disciples, 'I have been given all authority in heaven and on earth.'" It is here we understand the authority and the power by which we will share the gospel.

If we skip over verse 18 and go straight to verse 19—as happens all too often when the Great Commission is cited—it's easy to start thinking that "go and make disciples of all the nations" is something we're commanded to do on our own. But nothing could be further from the truth.

The gospel has power. It has the authority of Christ. When we obediently share the gospel, it is the power of the Holy Spirit that will convict and transform. "When he comes, he will convict the world of its sin, and of God's righteousness, and of the coming judgment" (John 16:8). Our role is simply to be obedient. As God has done with me on countless occasions, he can take your verbal shortcomings and uncertainties and use them for his purpose and his glory.

We can rest in these words of Jesus that conclude the Great Commission: "Be sure of this: I am with you always, even to the end of the age" (Matthew 28:20).

THE KINGDOM THAT HAS COME AND WILL COME

I wish I had paid more attention in my world history classes in high school and college. I particularly wish I had focused more on the different reigns and kingdoms, even more than the geopolitical entities we now call countries or nations. I could have been much better informed about the rich cultures that make up our world today.

Instead, I resorted to rote memorization because I knew the teacher would test us on dates, names, and basic facts. My goal was always to get a good grade, rather than focusing on getting a good education. As I have gotten older, I have attempted to make up for lost time. In fact, I recently completed a brief study of Portugal and Morocco, two nations relatively close in proximity but on two separate continents. I was amazed by how each country was profoundly shaped by different empires, kingdoms, and cultures.

But in the scope of eternity, there is only one kingdom that matters: the Kingdom of God. For certain, God has dominion over everything. After all, he is the creator. In the Bible, the Kingdom of God refers to God's redemptive rule of those who have been redeemed by the sacrifice of Jesus for us.

The Kingdom of God, then, is wherever believers in Jesus reside. When Paul wrote to the church at Colossae, he reminded them to be thankful and joyous because they now belonged to a new Kingdom: "He has rescued us from the kingdom of darkness and transferred us to the Kingdom of his dear Son, who purchased our freedom and forgave our sins" (Colossians 1:13-14).

When we share the gospel with others, we extend to them the offer of God to enter a new Kingdom, to submit to his reign and dominion. Such is the reason Jesus could proclaim boldly, "If I am casting out demons by the Spirit of God, then the Kingdom of God has arrived among you" (Matthew 12:28).

Although the Kingdom of God has arrived, it has not yet been completed. It is both "now" and "to come." The Kingdom has not yet been brought to its fulfillment. We look forward to the return of Christ and the completion of his Kingdom. We wait with expectation. We echo the words of the apostle John, who said, "He who is the faithful witness to all these things says, 'Yes I am coming soon!' Amen! Come, Lord Jesus!" (Revelation 22:20).

Evangelism is an invitation to enter the Kingdom that is and will be. When the rich man in Matthew 19:16 asks Jesus a basic question—"Teacher, what good deed must I do to have eternal life?"—Jesus explains the implications of giving up one's life to follow a new King. But "when the young man heard this, he went away sad, for he had many possessions" (Matthew 19:22). He wasn't ready to give up his current life for a life of following Jesus.

Later, Jesus took time to explain the encounter to his disciples: "I tell you the truth, it is very hard for a rich person to enter the Kingdom of Heaven. I'll say it again—it is easier for a camel to go through the eye of a needle than for a rich person to enter the Kingdom of God!" (Matthew 19:23-24).

The gospel is an invitation to leave our current kingdom to enter Christ's Kingdom. The place where God's Kingdom is demonstrated day by day is the church. Like God's people, no church is perfect. But it is where both new believers and longer-term believers join to show the world what Christ has done for them.

May we invite others into this gospel Kingdom. May we connect with other believers in churches around the world. Like the early church in Jerusalem, may we enjoy the goodwill of those outside the church. And may God add to our fellowship those who are being saved (Acts 2:47).

4

PRAYING . . . AND PRAYING SOME MORE

Prayer is the dividing line between those who share the gospel with ease and those who struggle to share the gospel, are afraid of sharing the gospel, or make excuses for not sharing the gospel. Let me state it even more bluntly: Prayer is the difference between Christians who share the gospel and Christians who don't.

I wrestled with where to place this chapter in the book. Because prayer is both the foundation and the centerpiece of evangelism, I wanted to feature it prominently. I thought of starting the book with a chapter on prayer, but I also thought it was important to deal up front with the importance of evangelism, the reasons for our uneasiness, and the essence of the gospel message. Consequently, chapter 4 became the first natural place in the flow of my argument to talk about prayer.

But please don't see the placement of this chapter as in any way minimizing the critical importance of prayer in evangelism. In fact, prayer may be the missing ingredient in evangelism for most Christians and in most churches. Evangelism without the undergirding power of prayer is evangelism without a power source.

CONNECTING TO THE POWER SOURCE

I have a confession to make: I recently purchased a robot vacuum cleaner. It wasn't on my list of most wanted items until I saw a friend's RoboVac in action. It's a pretty amazing device. You tap a button on your app and the machine moves around the room, cleaning until he (or she or it) is done.

Yes, my robot vacuum cleaner was pretty amazing—until it stopped working. It was as if it went on strike. A complete shutdown. Maybe it was tired of my incessant demands to clean the floor.

I tried different solutions on my own, but to no avail. Then I watched several YouTube videos, but the online experts were unable to solve my problem. As a last resort, I put aside all my pride and called the 800 number for the manufacturer's helpline. I really hate asking for directions.

The technician was very helpful. He even had me turn on my smartphone's video camera so he could see the issue live in my home. But it was his first question that got me a little irritated: "Is the charger plugged in?"

I was tempted to be snarky and ask him what a plug is, but I held back. To be fair, the technician probably talks to a dozen people a day who have simply forgotten to plug in their device. And though it wasn't true of me on this occasion, I have to admit that there have been times when I have overlooked the most basic and obvious solutions.

Plugging in to the power source is a pretty good metaphor for prayer. It's not a perfect metaphor—God's power includes a lot more than simply juice to drive a motor—but it will suffice for our purposes. Simply stated, we are disobedient and ineffective in our evangelism when we do not connect our efforts with the source of power God provides to reach people with the gospel.

When we truncate the Great Commission and start with "therefore, go and make disciples of all the nations," it's like pushing a car up a hill without an engine, brakes, and steering wheel. The car may look nice, but it's not going anywhere.

As we noted earlier, the Great Commission begins with the *authority* and *power* of Jesus Christ: "Jesus came and told his disciples, 'I have been given all authority in heaven and on earth'" (Matthew 28:18). And it ends with the promise of his *presence*: "And be sure of this: I am with you always, even to the end of the age" (Matthew 28:20).

Power, *authority*, and *presence*. Jesus wanted his disciples to understand clearly that sharing the gospel is not a human-centered endeavor; it is a Christ-sanctioned, Christ-empowered, Christ-infused endeavor.

After his resurrection and just before his ascension, Jesus told his followers to wait for the coming power of the Holy Spirit: "You will receive power when the Holy Spirit comes upon you. And you will be my witnesses, telling people about me everywhere—in Jerusalem, throughout Judea, in Samaria, and to the ends of the earth" (Acts 1:8).

Yet how many times have we heard Christians quote Acts 1:8 without the first sentence? How often do we talk about the mandate to *go* without mentioning the promise of power? Evangelism begins with the power of God through his Holy Spirit.

PRAY TO THE LORD OF THE HARVEST

In Matthew 9, Jesus is traveling through nearby towns and villages, sharing the Good News about the Kingdom of God. He also shows his followers a pattern of evangelism for them (and us) to emulate.

In the midst of these travels, Jesus becomes concerned about the large crowds that are asking for his help. The need is exceedingly great. Matthew 9:36-38 describes the scene: "When he saw the crowds, he had compassion on them because they were confused and helpless, like sheep without a shepherd. He said to his disciples. 'The harvest is great, but the workers are few. So pray to the Lord who is in charge of the harvest; ask him to send more workers into his fields.'"

The implications of these few sentences are massive. First, Jesus makes it abundantly clear that there is no shortage of people to reach. On more than one occasion, I've heard church leaders and church members say that there is no one to reach in their communities. But I have never been *anywhere* where there wasn't a harvest of souls to be reached. If we don't know any lost people, we need to broaden our circles. There will always be many to reach. Jesus was absolutely clear about that.

Second, Jesus tells us that one of the most important evangelistic prayers we can pray is for God to send more workers into the harvest. We are to pray for more people who are willing to share the gospel. This prayer is a mandate from Jesus. How many Christians pray this prayer regularly and faithfully? How many churches pray this prayer regularly and faithfully?

Third, how many Christians and churches understand that they are part of the answer to their own prayers? Clearly, if we are praying for God to send more workers into the harvest field, we should certainly be praying that we will be found faithful as well. The point is not to pray for *others* to share the gospel. We must pray that God will send us out to work side by side with those other workers.

Finally, note that Jesus refers to these harvest fields as *his* fields. God is already there. His Spirit is already working. We must simply be obedient and willing to share the gospel where God is already at work.

PRAY BECAUSE EVANGELISM IS SPIRITUAL WARFARE

Satan doesn't want us to share the gospel. He doesn't want to see people become citizens of the Kingdom of God. He wants them for himself. The enemy will do everything in his power to stop evangelism. Beginning the well-known "armor of God" passage in Ephesians 6:10-20, Paul describes the battle we are fighting:

> Be strong in the Lord and in his mighty power. Put on all of God's armor so that you will be able to stand firm against all strategies of the devil. For we are not fighting against flesh-and-blood enemies, but against evil rulers and authorities of the unseen world, against mighty powers in this dark world, and against evil spirits in the heavenly places.
>
> EPHESIANS 6:10-12

Paul then describes each piece of armor: the belt of truth; the body armor of God's righteousness; the shoes of peace; the shield of faith; the helmet of salvation; and the sword of the Spirit, which is the Word of God.

But don't miss how the passage ends. After detailing the armor of God, Paul reaches a crescendo with a great need: *prayer*. In verses 18-20, he states his case:

> Pray in the Spirit at all times and on every occasion. Stay alert and be persistent in your prayers for all believers everywhere. And pray for me, too. Ask God to give me the right words so I can boldly explain God's mysterious plan that the Good News is for Jews and Gentiles alike. . . . Pray that I will keep on speaking boldly for him, as I should.

Paul recognizes that the battle is first and foremost a spiritual one. He clearly states that his mission is to get the gospel to Jews and Gentiles alike. And he knows he needs prayer in order to fight this battle and get the message out. For Paul, and for us, evangelism is spiritual warfare. He asks for prayer for the right words as he shares the gospel. He recognizes the battle and knows what is at stake.

Evangelism without prayer is evangelism without power. When we obediently share the gospel with others, we confront hell's forces head-on. We must depend on God for his power. We must ask him for his protection, his words, and his open doors. We ask him through prayer.

PRAY FOR COURAGE

Though my first witnessing experience happened decades ago, I still remember my sweaty palms, racing heartbeat, and the lump in my throat that would not go away. Why is it that evangelism can cause such fear for some of us? Are we uncertain about the other person's reaction? Do we fear rejection? Are we not comfortable with our ability to share the gospel?

This book's title, *Sharing the Gospel with Ease*, would have been laughable to me when I went on my first evangelistic visit. There was no way I was at ease. To the contrary, I was a nervous wreck.

I know many Christians who do not have a problem talking about their faith. It is so incredibly natural for them. I thank God for people like that. In fact, I confess the sin of envy.

For the rest of us, evangelism takes courage. We cannot do it naturally. But we can do it supernaturally.

The story of Joshua preparing to lead Israel into the Promised Land has some parallels to evangelism. The people were getting ready to go where they had not been before. And though God had promised he would be with his people, there was still the uncertainty of the unknown.

When we share the gospel, we are inviting people to a Promised Land called the Kingdom of God.

What was the main message God had for Joshua as he led the people into a new land? It was simple: "Be strong and courageous. . . . Be strong and very courageous" (Joshua 1:6-7).

God repeats his message in Joshua 1:9 and adds a key promise: "This is my command—be strong and courageous! Do not be afraid or discouraged. For the LORD your God is with you wherever you go."

One of our prayers for sharing the gospel is simply a prayer for courage. For those of us who are not spiritual extroverts, the challenge can appear daunting. God, however, makes it clear. He wants us to have courage. And, he reminds us, he will be with us wherever we go.

What more could we ask for?

Pray for courage.

PRAY FOR OPPORTUNITIES

On the one hand, we don't need to pray for opportunities in the sense that we hope we can find some people who need to hear the gospel. Remember what Jesus said about the crowds, in Matthew 9:37: "The harvest is great, but the workers are few."

The harvest field is all around us. I have a Mormon

neighbor, a Hindu neighbor, and an agnostic neighbor. I only have to walk a few feet outside my front door to enter my mission field. When the COVID lockdown hit in 2020, most people spent a lot of time in their homes and neighborhoods. I was amazed at how many non-Christians were in my immediate vicinity. As I strolled the sidewalks of my neighborhood, I had opportunities for (socially distanced) conversations with my neighbors. As I got out of my house and got to know my neighbors better, many of these conversations led to spiritual discussions.

At Church Answers, we help churches understand their neighborhoods better by providing them with reports of their communities' demographics and psychographics. We ask church leaders to tell us the typical drive time of those who attend their worship services and then give them a description of their neighbors.

Demographics tell you *who* the people are. How many live within the typical driving distance for your church? What is the average income for the area? What is the typical family unit in the area? What is the racial and ethnic mix? How fast is the community growing? How fast has the community grown in the past?

Psychographics describe the *needs and desires* of the people in the community. What are their dreams? How many prefer a certain religious belief? What are some of their greatest physical and emotional needs?

When we present our reports to church leaders and members, we often hear two expressions of surprise. First, they may be surprised by the number of people who live within the typical driving distance. In one of our consultations, we asked the church leaders to guess how many people lived within a ten-minute drive of the church. The estimates ranged from 5,000 to 30,000. The actual population of the designated area was 250,000.

The second surprise is the estimated number of non-Christians who live within the typical driving distance. Even in rural churches, most leaders and members are shocked by the size of the mission field immediately around their church's address.

The point is simple but important: The mission field is *large* and *close*. There are more people than you could reach in a lifetime, and they live in your neighborhood.

Our prayer for opportunities is more that we would *see* the opportunities all around us. And once we've seen the needs, we should pray for courage as we move toward those opportunities.

I have challenged myself on many occasions to pray a prayer like this one: "Lord, give me eyes to see the opportunities to share the gospel today." Frankly, I can hardly remember a day when that prayer has not been answered.

Though it doesn't snow much in Nashville, as I've gotten older I have come to prefer the warmer climate of southwest

Florida for many weeks during the winter. On a trip to Bradenton, Florida, I prayed for an opportunity one morning to share the gospel. Within minutes, I received a text message from one of my neighbors. She wanted to know if I would join her and her husband for dinner that night.

The timing seemed more than coincidental. I wondered whether God was answering my prayer that quickly. At dinner, both of my neighbors asked me numerous spiritual questions. Though they had no religious affiliation, I could tell they were looking for something more. I hope I was faithful in my responses. I know God was faithful in providing me the opportunity to share the gospel within minutes of my prayer.

Praying for opportunities is a powerful prayer. God will put you in situations you never expected. You will find yourself talking to neighbors, merchants, physicians, restaurant servers, pizza delivery people, and many more. God will show you how vast the harvest fields truly are.

He simply wants willing workers. He wants you.

I am convinced that a neophyte in sharing the gospel could become a powerful evangelistic instrument with this simple prayer. I am convinced that the evangelistic apathy pervasive in many of our churches could turn to a hot gospel initiative with this prayer.

Would you consider pausing for a moment and praying a prayer similar to the one I mentioned above?

"Lord, give me eyes to see the opportunities to share the gospel today."

Perhaps if you pray that prayer today and continue in the days ahead, God will open your eyes to opportunities that are right in front of you. Then pray for courage to go to those whom God has shown you.

The harvest is great, but the workers are few.

Consider becoming a daily worker in the harvest field. And pray for other workers to join you.

PRAY FOR YOUR WALK WITH CHRIST

Social media is both a blessing and a bane.

I love it to keep up with friends and family. I find myself eagerly going to the sites of my sons and daughters-in-law to keep up with them and my grandchildren. I can't imagine not seeing photos of my grandchildren on a regular basis.

Social media is also a blessing when I'm looking for information of interest to me. Though I know that browser tracking and behavioral targeting can be creepy and have a Big Brother feel, I'm mostly appreciative of the filtering and curating that the social media sites provide. I would hate to think how difficult it would be to find something of interest without it. In fact, social media often points me to areas of interest I didn't know I had.

But social media is a bane as well. The watching world

sees Christians eviscerating one another over politics, music styles, Bible translations, and countless other issues. During the pandemic, the world saw us attack one another over matters of masks, social distancing, and when/whether to open for worship services.

It got ugly.

When the apostle Peter wrote his first letter, he was acutely aware that the world was watching Christians in the first century. His inspired writings apply just as powerfully today. He first exhorts believers not to succumb to worldly desires: "Dear friends, I warn you as 'temporary residents and foreigners' to keep away from worldly desires that wage war against your very souls" (1 Peter 2:11).

His admonishment reminds us not to get too comfortable with the things of this world. We are to live as temporary residents preparing for an eternal home.

Peter continues with the clear warning about our behavior in front of the watching world: "Be careful to live properly among your unbelieving neighbors. Then even if they accuse you of doing wrong, they will see your honorable behavior, and they will give honor to God when he judges the world" (1 Peter 2:12).

Our evangelistic witness is either enhanced or hindered by our behavior. Though we won't attain perfection in this life, we can make every effort in God's power to live lives that are honoring to him as the world watches us.

As I described earlier, my high school football coach, Joe Hendrickson, was a faithful witness who had an eternal influence on me. But there is more to the story.

Do you know why I hung on every word Coach Joe said when he called me into his office that day? Sure, he was my coach and had authority over me. To some extent, he had my attention because his position warranted it. But there was much more to it than that.

Coach Joe ultimately had my attention because I respected him and the life he lived. Sure, he was tough. Yes, he raised his voice on the practice field. But nothing he did was ever inappropriate. To the contrary, his life pointed me to Christ even when I may not have been consciously aware of it. One incident in particular stands out.

As a reminder, my time with Coach Joe was in the early 1970s in south Alabama. Racism was rampant. It is hard to convey in words the racial tensions and injustices of that time and place. African Americans were marginalized, chastised, and often persecuted. The governor of Alabama back then was George C. Wallace, whose platform was based on segregation. In his first inaugural address, in 1963, Governor Wallace emphatically declared that he stood for "segregation now, segregation tomorrow, and segregation forever."[4]

That was the environment in which I was raised. The schools had moved toward greater integration, but my first season with Coach Joe was the first time a few African

Americans joined the football team. It was not a popular decision among the white community.

What was amazing about Coach Joe was his calm demeanor and his equal treatment of all the players, black or white. But I'll never forget how, during the first week of practice, he approached a black player to explain a play to him. As he spoke to him, Coach Joe put his arm around the player's shoulders. Though the gesture was almost inconsequential to Coach Joe and wouldn't have drawn a lick of attention if the player had been white, it sent shock waves through the team and ultimately through our community.

But that was Coach Joe. He cared about his players, he treated everyone with respect, and it was genuine. So when he began sharing the gospel with me, he had my total attention. Indeed, he had my complete respect. I not only wanted to hear what he had to say, I wanted what he had in his life.

When we become believers in Christ, the Holy Spirit comes to dwell within us. The Spirit gives us the ability to live lives that are a powerful witness for Jesus even before we utter a word. Look at these words from 1 John 2:5-6: "Those who obey God's word truly show how completely they love him. That is how we know we are living in him. Those who say they live in God should live their lives as Jesus did."

Our prayer life as it connects to evangelism can take many paths. But we should not forget to pray for ourselves to become more like Jesus. The more clearly people can see

Jesus in us, the more opportunities we will have to share the gospel.

The Philippian jailer introduced in Acts 16:23 probably heard the gospel directly from Paul and Silas, but he seemed more profoundly affected by the witness of their lifestyle. He had no doubt heard them praying and singing hymns even after they had been beaten with wooden rods, thrown into the dungeon, and had their feet placed in wooden stocks (Acts 16:22-25). But that was only the beginning. When an earthquake opened the doors of the jail and removed the prisoners' chains, the jailer assumed that Paul and Silas and others had escaped, so he drew his sword to kill himself.

The text tells the powerful story in Acts 16:28-30: "Paul shouted to him, 'Stop! Don't kill yourself! We are all here!' The jailer called for lights and ran to the dungeon and fell down trembling before Paul and Silas. Then he brought them out and asked, 'Sirs, what must I do to be saved?'"

The jailer must have been affected by the gospel message and the singing of hymns. He must have been affected by the miracle of the earthquake. But he was clearly affected by the lives of Paul and Silas.

For many years, there was a debate among Christians about the efficacy of lifestyle evangelism versus a spoken witness. The Bible knows no such dichotomy. Evangelism is most effective when a person's lifestyle matches his or her words. The Philippian jailer both *heard* the gospel and *saw* the gospel. The same was true for me with Coach Joe Hendrickson. I saw the gospel and I heard the gospel.

PRAY FOR LOST LOVED ONES

I've known Chuck Lawless for more than twenty-five years. We have served together in a number of roles. Most important, he is a close friend whom I admire greatly.

Chuck has written extensively on prayer and spiritual warfare. He is invited to speak on these topics on a regular basis. He is truly a leading scholar in these fields.

But Chuck is not merely a scholar; he is a devout and prayerful man of God. His prayer life is exemplary; his witness is consistent.

I've known Chuck to pray for me and many others. Indeed, he is one of the first people we seek when we have a prayer need. We know Chuck will pray for us.

I have often heard Chuck talk about his own need for prayer. For example, his heart was broken for many years because his parents were not believers. He prayed for them faithfully and consistently. He wanted them to know the joy and hope that he has.

For a long time, it seemed those prayers would go unanswered. But Chuck persisted. Finally, after Chuck had prayed for thirty-six years, his dad became a follower of Christ at age seventy-one. And then, just a few months ago,

Chuck shared with me that his mother also accepted Christ as her Lord and Savior, at age seventy-nine, after her son had prayed for her salvation for forty-seven years. In his voice, I heard thanksgiving, joy, and great relief. It had been one of his greatest burdens.

Evangelism is for the world. But we must not forget that the world includes our own family members. As we pray for opportunities to share the gospel, we must also pray fervently for loved ones who are not yet Christians.

In addition to our prayers, our lifestyle in the presence of our loved ones must demonstrate the life and love of Jesus. And though we're not perfect—and our loved ones know that better than anyone—they should be able to see something different about us. Eventually, they may even ask the same question posed by the Philippian jailer: "What must I do to be saved?"

In the case of Chuck Lawless's mom, both he and his dad were influences on her. In fact, she commented that the change she saw in her husband was instrumental in her decision. She saw the peace he had. She saw how God had conquered his temper problem. She saw how he devoured the Scriptures.

She saw Christ in him.

Prayer is foundational to our evangelistic efforts with our loved ones. Indeed, prayer is instrumental in *all* our evangelism.

By now, you get the point. Sharing the gospel with ease means we do not depend on our own power, but on the power of God. And there is simply no better way to connect ourselves to God's power than through prayer.

Do you really want to share the gospel with ease? There is no more powerful and effective way than to make certain you are praying as an indispensable part of your evangelistic efforts.

Evangelism without prayer is indeed evangelism without power.

5

WHAT EXACTLY SHOULD WE SAY?

My wife, Nellie Jo, was a wonderful actress in high school. For two consecutive years, she was named the outstanding actress in the state for her leading roles in two plays. Though she does not regret the path she took in life, away from the theater, I know God would have blessed her greatly had she chosen to stay in the world of acting. She was just that good.

I had been dating Nellie Jo for a few months when I went to watch her perform in a play during her junior year of high school. The drama department at our high school was new, so I didn't know what to expect. To say I was blown away would be an understatement.

The play was incredible. It was hard to believe those were teenagers performing onstage. They truly melded into their respective characters, and I forgot they were people I knew personally.

But Nellie Jo was the best. She totally commanded her character. I got lost in the play and forgot for a few moments that it was my girlfriend up there on the stage. (Okay, I remembered quite clearly when she kissed the leading actor.)

I'm always amazed when I watch any exceptional actor or actress. I know I am in the presence of great talent when I become totally immersed in the story and forget that it is actors acting. How do they adopt completely different personalities in their acting roles? How are they able to set aside who they are and be someone else?

We all know people who have pretentious personalities, who try to act like someone other than who they are. These are not actors or actresses on a stage or in a movie. They are pretenders who are disguising their true selves for less than noble reasons.

For some reason, many Christians undergo a personality change that is both obvious and off-putting when they share the gospel.

Some of this might be attributable to simple nervousness. It's not unusual for someone who has rarely shared the gospel to be fearful or uncertain. I've been there and done that. Persistent obedience and experience will take care of that problem over time.

Some Christians, though, exude a false piety when

discussing spiritual things. They create a "holy façade" when they talk about Jesus. Most non-Christians see through that guise quickly and easily. In the common vernacular, it's known as being "holier than thou."

But we don't need a personality transplant to tell someone about Jesus. We have the most authentic message in history. We have the gospel. We just need to be ourselves and allow the light of Christ to shine through us.

I think about the conversations I have that come naturally. Sometimes, if you get me talking about my family, you can't get me to stop. You've already heard what I think about Nellie Jo, and I can go on at length as well about my children (including three incredible daughters-in-law) and my eleven grandchildren (as of this writing—I'll keep you posted if we add more). From the day my three sons were born, I was totally smitten with them and the honor of being their dad. I still feel honored now that they are grown men.

I love talking about my organization, Church Answers. I am passionate about our ministry and the opportunities our team has. I love the members of our team. They are like a second family to me.

And though I won't mention any specific team, I can get pretty excited about college football. I particularly enjoy talking to other fans of my team.

Do you know what distinguishes those conversations? I'm just being myself. I don't undergo a personality change. I don't sound pious or contrived. Sure, I can get pretty enthusiastic about any of these topics, but I don't become a different person when I talk about them.

So why should I adopt a different personality when I talk about Jesus? People recognize sincerity and transparency. They also recognize when someone is faking it.

I remember a student in my class at seminary who shared about his witnessing experience. He told us he had asked God to let him share the gospel in his own natural way. He asked for opportunities that would flow from the normal walk of his life. God answered those prayers. This young man reported that conversations were easy and flowed from his personality as God used him. He observed how calm he was and how naturally the conversations ensued. In short, he shared the gospel with ease.

Be yourself when you talk about Jesus. Share from your own experience in a way that is consistent with your natural personality. Be genuine when sharing the gospel. Be humble. God will supply the right words at the right time using the right person—*you*.

THE POWER OF YOUR STORY

Many times, the best way to share the gospel is to tell your own story. Stories stick. Stories have power.

Brian was a member of my church many years ago when

I was a pastor. He came back from the Vietnam War with many issues. I guess they would be called post-traumatic stress disorder today. Brian's challenges included illegal drug use, alcohol abuse, and a host of physical and psychological problems. In his own words, he was "a living train wreck."

Then Brian became a Christian.

If you expect me to say that every challenge he faced went away immediately, I must disappoint you. He continued to struggle in many areas. But he did change. And even though he continued to experience setbacks, everyone who knew him saw dramatic improvement.

Brian had one very positive attribute as a Christian: He was totally excited about his faith and he wanted the world to know. His enthusiasm reminded me of Peter and John when they appeared before the Sanhedrin in Acts 4:20: "We cannot stop telling about everything we have seen and heard."

That was Brian. He couldn't stop talking about Jesus. Over time, he learned how God could use his story in powerful ways. When he encountered a skeptic, he was able to honestly say that he'd had the same perspective before Christ came into his life. On other occasions, when he encountered people that most would call outcasts, he would tell them his story and say that if Jesus could save him, he could save them, too.

His story was dramatic and powerful.

The apostle Paul used his own conversion story in similarly powerful ways, such as in his appeal to Agrippa:

> I used to believe that I ought to do everything
> I could to oppose the very name of Jesus the
> Nazarene. Indeed, I did just that in Jerusalem.
> Authorized by the leading priests, I caused many
> believers there to be sent to prison. And I cast my
> vote against them when they were condemned to
> death. Many times I had them punished in the
> synagogues to get them to curse Jesus. I was so
> violently opposed to them that I even chased them
> down in foreign cities.
>
> ACTS 26:9-11

Paul's conversion on the road to Damascus was as dramatic as it gets. So was his "before and after" story.

But you may wonder whether your story has any value in sharing the gospel. Compared to Paul's and Brian's, you may think your story is boring and predictable. Not at all.

The best examples I can give you are my three sons, Sam, Art, and Jess. They all have conversion stories that happened at a relatively young age. Since they were the sons of a pastor and a godly mother, you would expect that they had every opportunity to hear and respond to the gospel.

All three of my sons became followers of Christ. In fact,

all three are in vocational ministry today. But each has his own story. They all became aware that they were sinners and could not save themselves. And they all knew they had to believe in Christ and turn from their sins. They could not appropriate my faith, or Nellie Jo's faith, and claim it by right of inheritance. Each had to trust Christ for himself, individually and personally.

The point is, no matter what your background, there was a time when you stepped out of darkness and into the light of Christ. Every story of a transformed life is powerful. *Your* story is powerful, and God will use it in many ways. Your story may have drama, like Brian's and Paul's stories. Or your story may be one of coming to realize that having grown up in a Christian home couldn't save you—that *all* have sinned and fall short of God's glory—and you had to make your own decision for Christ. Every story can and will be used by God. When you tell others what Christ has done for you, you are sharing the gospel through your own testimony.

REMEMBER TO SHARE THE CONTENT OF THE GOSPEL

It is vital, of course, that you share the truth of the gospel. Jesus came to earth as fully God and fully human. His mission was to save the lost. He lived a sinless life. He went to the cross as the only righteous substitute for our sins. He died and his body was placed in a tomb. On the third day, he rose from the dead and defeated death. He lived on earth for forty days after his resurrection. Then he ascended to heaven and now sits at the right hand of God the Father. If we truly confess and repent of our sins and place our faith in Jesus, he will forgive us and give us eternal life.

Yes, the complete gospel narrative is a bit long for a brief conversation. Maybe you will have time to share all of it; at other times you may have to be more concise.

Remember the story of the Philippian jailer in Acts 16? Amid the chaos of an earthquake that shook the entire prison, sprung open the doors, and released the chains of the prisoners, the jailer thought he was doomed and decided to take his own life. As he drew his sword to kill himself, Paul and Silas shouted to him to stop, that all the prisoners were still in their cells.

When the jailer, greatly relieved, asked them, "What must I do to be saved?" Paul and Silas did not launch into a long discourse about the essence of the gospel. They simply and quickly responded, "Believe in the Lord Jesus and you will be saved, along with everyone in your household" (Acts 16:30-31).

Responding to the jailer's question, Paul and Silas began with the first, most fundamental step: *believe*. Later, after the jailer had invited them into his home and brought his family around, Paul and Silas expanded on their initial exhortation to the jailer as they "shared the word of the Lord with him and with all who lived in his household" (Acts 16:32).

The point is simple: Take every opportunity to share as much of the content of the gospel as the situation allows, and make every effort to follow up to explain the truth in greater breadth and depth. You don't want to abbreviate the truth of the gospel so much that your hearer has an incomplete view of Christ's work, but don't pass up an opportunity to share the gospel just because you don't have time to completely disciple someone. Remember, it is the Holy Spirit who "will convict the world of its sin, and of God's righteousness, and of the coming judgment" (John 16:8). Your role is to faithfully present the truth of the gospel with as much content as the situation will allow. In the case of Paul and Silas, they left town the next day after being released from prison. But not before they "returned to the home of Lydia [where] they met with the believers and encouraged them once more" (Acts 16:40). Having faithfully shared the gospel with the jailer and his family, they entrusted their further growth to the Holy Spirit working through the other believers in Philippi.

I have heard many Christians share testimonies of a "false salvation," based on being told that all they had to do was "accept Jesus" in their hearts and they would be saved. Though many have truly responded to such an abbreviated gospel and later were taught the full gospel of repentance and faith, many others only recited words they were told to repeat and went on with their lives unchanged, holding to a false assurance of salvation.

No matter what we say when we share the gospel, in the end we must simply trust the Holy Spirit to take our words and make an eternal difference in the lives of the people to whom we witness. Here's a beautiful truth: We don't have to depend on our own strength, power, or wisdom to share the gospel. We don't have to worry about messing up when we speak. God's Spirit does the work of saving people. He will be with us and guide us as we speak, even as we speak out of our own weakness.

THE HOLY SPIRIT WORKS IN OUR WEAKNESS

I cringe when I recall some of my tepid attempts at sharing the gospel. Do you remember the story I told about Jim in chapter 2? That was the time when I opened my mouth and these words flowed out: "Jim, you don't want to go to hell, do you?"

Ouch. My face still turns red whenever I think about that blunder, even though it was decades ago. How much more could I have gotten wrong? I didn't mention Jesus or his sinless life. I said nothing about his death on the cross for our sins. And not a word about his resurrection or the need for repentance and faith.

But you know the rest of the story. God took my nervous

obedience and highly inadequate words and used them to open the door. When Jim asked me how he could go to heaven, I had a second chance to present the robust content of the gospel.

To be clear, our dependence on the Holy Spirit is not an excuse for laziness or lack of preparation. It is, however, a reminder that the words we speak are generated in God's power and not our own.

SOMETIMES QUESTIONS HELP

We sometimes make the mistake of thinking of evangelism as a one-way street. That is, we make our best attempt at presenting a clear gospel message and the other person either responds or doesn't respond. But presenting the gospel with ease often includes asking questions. In fact, when we ask questions, it shows we are interested in the other person's perspective. It's a sign of respect, and it can help us target our message in words that the other person can more easily receive. Questions may also open the door to a fuller presentation of the gospel.

The story of Philip and the Ethiopian eunuch is enlightening. Hearing the man reading aloud from the prophet Isaiah, Philip's first words are a question: "Do you understand what you are reading?" (Acts 8:30).

Look how the story unfolds. "The man replied, 'How

can I, unless someone instructs me?' And he urged Philip to come up into the carriage and sit with him" (Acts 8:31).

Philip seizes the opportunity. "The eunuch asked Philip, 'Tell me, was the prophet talking about himself or someone else?' So beginning with the same Scripture, Philip told him the Good News about Jesus" (Acts 8:34-35).

But don't miss how this encounter began. The eunuch was seated in his carriage when the Holy Spirit said to Philip, "Go over and walk along beside the carriage" (Acts 8:29). God provided the opportunity and the Holy Spirit prompted Philip to take action. Philip obeyed, engaging the man with the gospel of Christ through a question.

The questions we ask don't have to be intimidating or intrusive. For example, the simple question, "When you attend church, where do you usually go?" allows the person an opportunity to talk about religious matters without feeling judged by their response. Most people have attended a church at some point in their lives, if only for a funeral, a wedding, or a special Christmas presentation. But even if they've never darkened the doors of a church, asking the question gives you more information to go on. You might follow up with something like this: "Oh, that's interesting. Tell me more about your background." And now you're in a conversation.

At Church Answers, I have the opportunity to research Christianity and church trends. When I tell someone my background, I'm able to follow up with a question, asking for their help: "What do you think when you hear the word *Christian*?"

Of course, I have to be prepared for some challenging responses because many people have negative views of Christians. People often tell me the crazy and sad things some Christians say on social media.

As long as I'm not defensive when they respond, we are usually able to engage in a vibrant conversation about matters of faith. And if I can demonstrate that I am not like the crazy Christians on social media, I may have even more opportunities to share my faith.

When we witness, we do not have to dominate the conversation. In fact, if we are genuinely concerned about other people, we want to hear their stories. We want to hear their opinions. As part of your preparation, take a journey through the New Testament. See how Jesus uses questions to engage people. See how he moves people to answer their own questions by asking even more questions.

The power of asking questions is that it draws the other person out. You're there to listen, not lecture. You're there to affirm and encourage as much as possible. When you demonstrate genuine care and concern through your questions, doors will open for even more questions and for more opportunities to share the gospel.

EXPECT OPENNESS

There is a sense among many Christians that most non-Christians are resistant to, or even adversarial about, discussing the gospel. They base their assumptions on what they've read on social media or in the news. Perhaps they've heard about or experienced an occasional harsh response, and thus are basing their opinion on a one-in-a-hundred conversation.

Christians too often become defensive or fearful when discussing matters of faith with non-Christians. Yes, the exclusivity of the gospel can be offensive to some people. There will be those who recoil at the truth that there is only one way of salvation. But let's not write God out of the equation right from the start. We must anticipate that he is at work before us, preparing the harvest fields.

Simply stated, we should expect many people to be responsive to the words we share. We should be confident that God is already at work in their lives. But we must never compromise the content of the gospel for fear of a negative reaction from other people.

Let's return to Matthew 9:36-38 for a moment: "When [Jesus] saw the crowds, he had compassion on them because they were confused and helpless, like sheep without a shepherd. He said to his disciples, 'The harvest is great, but the workers are few. So pray to the Lord who is in charge of the harvest; ask him to send more workers into his fields.'"

As we noted earlier, the challenge is more with finding workers than with finding a receptive harvest field. That alone should make us very confident in communicating the gospel.

Another point that bears repeating is that Jesus identifies the place of harvest as *his fields*. The lost are already in his domain. God is already at work there. He wants us to do our part to bring in the harvest that awaits in his fields.

Several years ago, my research team and I conducted interviews with unchurched non-Christians.[5] Through a series of questions, we sought to determine their attitudes toward Christians, Christian beliefs, and churches in general. Much to our surprise, we found very few non-Christians— only 5 percent—who had an antagonistic attitude. Also surprising was the fact that we found a great deal of receptivity to the issues we asked about in our survey. Though our team approached the project with all the rigors of research, we came away encouraged and inspired about sharing the gospel. We discovered for ourselves what Jesus had already said. The harvest is indeed great.

TOOLS TO HELP YOU KNOW WHAT TO SAY

For several decades, we've had an abundance of tools available to teach us how to present the gospel, how to handle objections, and how to engage in conversations about the gospel. As I mentioned earlier, I was in my twenties before I ever shared the gospel with anyone. It was my fumbling of the opportunity to lead my friend Jim to Christ that drove me to seek more information and training.

I was a young businessman at the time, so I went directly to my pastor to ask him if there were any resources available to help me share the gospel more effectively. Sadly, he told me he didn't know much about evangelism. When he saw the dejected look on my face, he asked me to wait a minute. He said he thought he had received a free copy of a book on the subject. He didn't think he had thrown it away.

The book my pastor handed me was *Evangelism Explosion* by D. James Kennedy.[6] I had never seen anything like it. I later discovered that the program was used by churches and Christians around the world.

Though I never participated in formal Evangelism Explosion training, the book gave me a helpful framework for understanding evangelism. And though I adapted the program to better fit my personality and circumstances, it proved to be an immensely helpful tool. To this day, I still use some of the lessons from the book, especially the parts that answer the question, "What do I say?"

In our digital age, evangelistic tools in abundance are now available. I use the app called Life on Mission. It includes an illustration called 3 Circles, which is a simple way to have gospel conversations. I simply type an arrow on the app, and I can take a person through a robust gospel presentation.

In our efforts to share the gospel, we may not have the perfect words to say, but we do have a great number of tools to help us. These tools are not for everyone, but they have certainly helped me throughout my life.

COMMIT NOT TO BE A SILENT CHRISTIAN

I prefer to keep my mouth shut.

Seriously. I would rather listen to others than speak myself. It goes with my introverted personality. I rarely feel compelled to contribute to a conversation. Even when I think I have better solutions or ideas, I'm more apt to keep quiet.

Being an introvert is not a bad thing. It means I listen more, for one. I don't typically come across as a know-it-all with an opinion on every subject. And when I keep my mouth shut, I don't put my ignorance on display for the world to see.

But when it comes to sharing the gospel, silence is not an option. We must speak up. It is a sin to be silent when God has commanded us to speak. I must be reminded of that truth daily. And I must recommit myself to that truth regularly.

May I suggest a fivefold prayer of commitment (or recommitment) to prepare yourself for speaking up and sharing the gospel? I'm convinced God will answer this prayer if it reflects your heart's desire.

First, pray to get your priorities in order. Sometimes, we are too busy for our own good and don't have time for obedience to God. The tyranny of the urgent replaces God's priority of the moment. We are so busy doing life that we fail to do life as God intended. If we could really grasp the importance of our evangelistic mandate, we would always make it a priority.

More than seven thousand people die every hour worldwide.[7] Are we concerned about where they will spend eternity? Are their souls a priority for us? How can we be silent when so many people need to hear the gospel?

Second, pray for reminders. I wish I were so close to God that I could see the world through his eyes every moment. But I'm not even close to being that close! I have to ask God for holy reminders. I need those providential prods to remind me not to keep my mouth shut.

A few years ago, I was in conversation with a very wealthy businessman. It was an intense discussion about a business deal with my company. I went into the meeting ready to discuss and negotiate. I thought I had my facts together and was well prepared.

Then I received a godly nudge. I knew I was supposed to ask him if he was a Christian. Yes, I was supposed to change the subject from an intense business transaction to the business of God. So I did. His response was scattered, but clear to me. He was not a Christian. From that point forward, I saw him through different eyes. I spoke more openly about my relationship with Christ.

The businessman and I have since gone our separate ways, and I don't know if he ever became a Christian. I can only pray that God used our conversations to move him closer to a decision.

Third, we must pray for opportunities to speak. As I've mentioned, I know of countless situations where God honored the prayers of faithful Christians who prayed for opportunities. Whether he set people in their paths or opened their eyes to the people already around them, I don't know. But the outcome was the same. A Christian became aware of an opportunity to share the gospel and took it.

Fourth, pray for the right words to fit the situation. Of course, God can use our imperfect attempts for his glory. He has certainly used my stumbling words on more than one occasion. But that doesn't mean we should be unprepared to speak. That doesn't mean we should settle for stumbling and bumbling. We can study the Bible more diligently to prepare. We can learn from others how to make our gospel conversations better and stronger. Even more, we can pray for the right words.

You may be confronted with the most difficult gospel conversation you could imagine. Your own intellect, wisdom, and strength may not give you the right words. But God can give you exactly what he wants you to say. You don't have to depend on your own insight and ability. God will answer your prayers. If you ask him and trust him, he will give you the words to say.

Fifth, and finally, pray for your own obedience. This prayer is really a summary of all our other prayers. We know we're supposed to share the gospel. We know we're supposed to speak up and not remain silent. We know we're supposed to be obedient. But sometimes we need to ask God to help us with our obedience.

A TIME TO SPEAK

Even though I'm more inclined to remain silent than to speak, there have been times when I've spoken but wish I had kept my mouth shut. There are comments and statements I've posted on social media that I'd like to have back. I've learned the wisdom of listening instead of debating or defending.

But God's mandate for us to share the gospel is clear. That's why I've chosen Acts 4:20 as my life verse: "We cannot stop telling about everything we have seen and heard." When Peter and John said those words to the ruling authorities, their very lives were at risk. The least I can do is to speak the gospel as God gives me opportunities. No one has ever threatened to kill me for sharing the gospel.

The writer of Ecclesiastes reminds us, "For everything there is a season, a time for every activity under heaven" (3:1). In that same context, he includes "a time to be quiet and a time to speak" (3:7).

For certain, there are times to be quiet. Many Christians would benefit by practicing those times more often.

But there is never a time to be quiet when the gospel is at stake. We must speak, and we must speak boldly. Indeed, it is a sin to be silent when God has commanded us to speak.

6

THOSE PESKY OBJECTIONS

I led my first church consultation in 1988. To be honest, I didn't even know I was doing a consultation. A pastor in my city simply asked me to look at his church and make some recommendations. I did the best I could and shared my opinions after observing his church for several days. He must have been pleased with my counsel, because he recommended me to several other churches that same year.

Over time, I developed a consulting ministry and have since worked with thousands of churches with a variety of requests and needs. I certainly remember my uncertainty and lack of confidence with the first few consultations. Everything was new, and everything was a challenge. The learning curve was steep.

To be clear, I don't have all the answers for churches today. Not even close. Yet, after consulting with churches for so many years, I see common patterns. I see recurring themes. Someone recently asked me if I could walk into a church facility and know exactly what they need to do within a few hours. Absolutely not. Every church consultation takes time and prayer. And God continues to surprise me when I work with churches.

If you share the gospel enough times, you will begin to see patterns. You will hear conversations you've heard before. You will grow in confidence and be better prepared to deal with objections. In fact, you'll hear some of the same objections over and over again. You might begin to view them as pesky.

But no matter how many times you hear the same objections, don't take them lightly. You are discussing someone's eternal life. You may have heard it all before, but for the person to whom you're speaking, that objection is real and personal and unique. You must deal with objections with compassion and grace.

I have had the same physician for more than fifteen years. He's an internist with brilliant diagnostic skills. He has become a friend over the years, and we enjoy talking with one another when I visit him.

For my most recent annual physical, I commented to him that he must get tired of hearing the same complaints of aches and pains day after day. Though I don't remember his exact response, he essentially told me that the day he doesn't care deeply about his patients is the day he needs to retire. Every physical concern is a unique burden to the patient, whether the doctor has heard it a thousand times or not.

My doctor's attitude of concern affected me deeply that day. And as I write this book about sharing the gospel, I'm acutely aware that we are dealing with people who have a sickness called sin. The only person who can solve their problem is someone we sometimes refer to as the Great Physician. People may have common objections. Those questions may seem pesky at times. But we must love them with the love of Christ. For them, every objection can be real and formidable.

There is no way to compile a list of every potential objection. I have seen some writers, though, compile a pretty impressive number of them. For now, let's just look at a few of the more common questions and concerns you will likely hear.

"I'M NOT A BAD PERSON"

People who use this objection typically see the path to heaven as a balance between good deeds and bad. As long as the scales tilt in their favor, they will be accepted into heaven. Pop culture often affirms this wrong theology.

Of course, we know that "everyone has sinned; we all fall short of God's glorious standard" (Romans 3:23). We know that any sin is offensive to a holy and perfect God. We know that the price of sin is death, and only Jesus, as our substitute on the cross, can save us from eternal separation from God.

But what do you say to the person who voices the objection, "I'm really not a bad person"?

You can certainly cite Romans 3:23. Many times the Holy Spirit will use Scripture to convict a person whose hope is riding on doing enough good deeds. I like to point to James 2:10: "The person who keeps all of the laws except one is as guilty as a person who has broken all of God's laws."

I will also explain that because God is perfect, no sin can come into his presence. The only way to come into God's presence is to have all of our sins forgiven.

I point to my own life as a sinner in need of forgiveness. I don't want to appear as if I think I'm any better than the other person. We're all in the same boat. We all need the same forgiveness of sins.

Another good approach is to tell the person the story of the three crosses from Scripture. Two of the crosses were occupied by criminals. The one in the middle was occupied by Jesus, the perfect, sinless man. Neither criminal deserved to go to heaven. Both were obviously pretty bad men to have been sentenced to crucifixion.

> One of the criminals hanging beside [Jesus] scoffed, "So you're the Messiah, are you? Prove it by saving yourself—and us, too, while you're at it!"

But the other criminal protested, "Don't you fear God even when you have been sentenced to die? We deserve to die for our crimes, but his man hasn't done anything wrong." Then he said, "Jesus, remember me when you come into your Kingdom."

And Jesus replied, "I assure you, today you will be with me in paradise."

LUKE 23:39-43

The criminal that Jesus pardoned certainly did not have the balance of good deeds on his side of the scale. It was only by his faith in Jesus that he got to heaven. No one will get to God by their own good works.

"I'VE DONE TOO MANY BAD THINGS"

This objection is the flip side of the good deeds argument.

Melody started attending a church in St. Petersburg, Florida, where I was serving as pastor. She epitomized the spiritual seeker. She knew something was missing in her life but didn't know what. One morning, she showed up at our church looking for the missing pieces.

I remember the first time I asked her if she was a Christian. Her response was different from anything I had heard: "I'm almost sure I'm not."

As I tried to unpack her answer, I began to understand

her unusual choice of words. Melody had no trouble believing in God, or at least some type of god. She was willing to accept Jesus for who he said he is.

But she had trouble accepting Jesus as her Lord and Savior because she wasn't convinced that Jesus would accept her.

Melody had been sexually abused by a relative when she was young. She had been married and divorced three times. Her only child belonged to none of her three former husbands. She'd had long bouts with drugs and alcohol. In short, she felt unworthy, dirty, and unforgivable.

A few ladies in our church began to mentor Melody. They pointed her to passages in Scripture that dealt with people who embraced Christ even though they had wrecked lives. They showed her that she was no more a sinner than anyone else. They pointed to passages that showed her Christ loved her even though she was a sinner.

Still, Melody struggled. Though she accepted the Bible stories as true and powerful, she had trouble accepting that they applied to her—or that anyone could love her, especially God.

Then one day, much to my surprise, Melody told me she was a Christian. She had repented of her sins and by faith accepted Jesus as her Lord and Savior. She wanted to be baptized.

I was shocked and delighted. I asked her simply, "What happened?"

"Those ladies refused to give up on me," she said. "Everyone else in my life that I tried to get close to would always leave me. I really expected them to walk away because I knew I didn't deserve their love."

She paused, with tears flowing unashamedly.

"But those four women would not stop loving me," she continued. "I tried to figure out why they were so different and then, one day, the light went on. They are different because they have Christ in their lives. He is real. He is forgiving. He does love me. I saw Christ for the first time in the lives of those four women."

Sometimes we can point to Scripture to show people how much God loves them—no matter how bad they think they are. Sometimes we can persuade them of that truth. But sometimes they can't be convinced until they *see* Jesus in the lives of others. We have to love them into the Kingdom. That was Melody's story. Those four women made an eternal difference.

"I'LL THINK ABOUT IT LATER"

I remember my friend Ryan from high school. We went to the same church, the same school, and played on the same sports teams. Before I became a Christian, Ryan was a big influence on me, but not in a good way.

Ryan was a rebel and a big partier during his teenage and college years. He liked his life the way it was and didn't want to give up the "good times." He completely believed the facts about Jesus. He believed that Jesus was the Son of God. He believed he died on the cross for our sins. He believed that Jesus rose from the dead and defeated death. He believed that Christ was the only way of salvation, and that only by grace through faith can we be saved.

But despite all he believed about Jesus, Ryan was unwilling to surrender his life to him. He preferred to gamble with his salvation, depending on a last-minute change of heart, or a deathbed confession, somewhere down the road. In the meantime, he chose to live life his own way, filled with rebellion and self-destructive behavior.

Not everyone is as transparent as Ryan. They don't see their objection as a gamble. Rather, they simply think they have time. They can make a decision for Christ later—maybe.

Objections like these are often difficult to challenge because people with this attitude may actually agree with the truth of the gospel and the truth of Scripture. They simply don't feel the urgency. Nor are they usually receptive to common-sense arguments. You can tell them that no one is guaranteed their next breath, and they will probably agree with you. Still, they are willing to gamble.

Three often-effective responses to this objection are not immediately apparent. First, as with all objections, we can and should pray for them to come to their senses. They must have a change of heart, the type of change that can only come through conviction by the Holy Spirit.

Second, if possible, we can pursue a friendship relationship with them. This approach, too, is valuable in dealing with almost any objection. The prayer and hope is that they will see the truth of Christ in your life and be drawn to it. They don't have to trade a life of so-called fun for a life of boring piety. Your life can show them that life in Christ is both joyous and fulfilling.

Third, you can be prepared when life shakes their foundations. Though we would never pray for tragedy or bad things to happen to someone, we all experience pain and heartache at some point in our lives. If you're there for them, particularly during tough times, their receptivity to the gospel may be enhanced. Maybe they will see their need for a Lord and Savior.

"HOW CAN A LOVING GOD LET BAD THINGS HAPPEN TO PEOPLE?"

When I was a young man in my twenties, my dad died from lung cancer. Dad was not only my hero; he was also my best friend. He meant the world to me.

I argued with God a lot about my dad's illness. I got mad at God on occasion. I bargained with God to spare my dad's life. As if God didn't know already, my dad had made a remarkable difference in the lives of many people. He had grown up quickly at age ten when his mother died and his father turned to alcohol. Though Dad saw many horrible things in World War II, he continued to fight for his country and for our freedoms.

My dad was progressive on race issues when racism was rampant in the south Alabama town where we lived. He stood up to a circuit judge named George Wallace, the same man who later became governor on a platform of segregation. My dad embraced the African American community when few other whites would go near them.

He adored my mom, my brother, and me. Why would God take him from us?

I was familiar with the theological concept of *theodicy*—from the Greek for "justifying God"—which seeks to explain why and how a good, perfect, almighty, and all-knowing God permits evil and bad things to happen to people. I understood the consequences of sin coming into the world and how it contributed to the problems we have—including illness and suffering. But I wanted God to make an exception for my dad. I knew God could do that. I had trouble understanding why he wouldn't.

I was a Christian then. In fact, I was a seminary student preparing for ministry. But I still struggled. Perhaps my faith should have been stronger, but I struggled.

I can only imagine, then, how tough it is for non-Christians. They typically don't know or care anything about the doctrine of theodicy. If they or someone they love needs help, they just want God to help. They don't want a lecture on original sin.

These situations are indeed challenging when sharing the gospel. My default mode has been to be pastoral and prayerful. I want hurting and questioning people to know I care. I know they often need to see the love of Christ in me before they will consider accepting Jesus as their Savior.

On occasion, someone has asked me specific biblical questions about theodicy. I do my best to show him or her how sin came into the world, and how it messes things up today. I point them to the day when there will be no pain and no more tears. But more times than not, I simply show love and compassion.

An issue related to theodicy is the doctrine of hell. How could a loving God send people to hell?

I gently remind those who ask this question that God doesn't desire for anyone to go to hell. Many times, I'll have them read 2 Peter 3:9: "The Lord isn't really being slow about his promise, as some people think. No, he is being patient for your sake. He does not want anyone to be destroyed, but wants everyone to repent."

Sometimes, when they read that last sentence and see that God doesn't want anyone to perish, their eyes light up. It becomes an open door to point to the love of God, perhaps through John 3:16, the most well-known verse in the Bible: "For this is how God loved the world: He gave his one and only Son, so that everyone who believes in him will not perish but have eternal life."

Such is the positive side of these objections. They can become open doors to share even more about the love of God. They become gospel pathways.

"THERE ARE MANY WAYS TO GET TO HEAVEN OR GOD"

Oprah Winfrey has declared on more than one occasion that there are multiple ways to God and heaven.[8] We should not be surprised when a cultural icon makes such a claim. There are many who struggle with the belief that Jesus is the only way to God.

The doctrine is called *exclusivity*, the biblical belief that Jesus is the only way to God—no exceptions whatsoever. This was not some belief that later followers of Jesus tacked on to a religious system; it is the very heart of Christianity. In fact, it was Jesus himself who made this claim. One of the most explicit passages, in Jesus' own words, is John 14:6-7: "I am the way, the truth, and the life. No one can come to the Father except through me. If you had really known me, you would know who my Father is. From now on, you do know him and have seen him!"

For many non-Christians, exclusivity is not only a stumbling block, it is offensive. "How can you be so narrowminded to say there is only one way?" one man asked a friend of mine. Exclusivity is the opposite of inclusivity, which is embraced by many in our culture today. We can and should expect opposition to this central Christian tenet.

It is not likely you can win a debate over this issue. People either believe it or they don't. Be certain you point to the words of Christ, particularly John 14:6. These people are not rejecting what *you* say; they are rejecting what Jesus said. Either Jesus told the truth that he is the only way to God, or he is a liar and unworthy of our faith. That's the choice we all have.

"I BELIEVE IN GOD"

What sounds like an affirmation at first can quickly become a denial. Many non-Christians will say they believe in God, but they really don't believe in the one true God revealed in the Bible through the person of Jesus Christ. Remember what it says in John 14:7: "If you had really known me, you would know who my Father is. From now on, you do know him and have seen him!"

God is Jesus. Jesus is God. Many people say they believe in God, but what they mean is that they believe in *a* god. How they view that god depends on many factors but it is obviously not the same God revealed in Jesus Christ.

Dealing with objections to the deity of Christ is similar to dealing with objections to the doctrine of exclusivity. We have an opportunity to point people directly to Scripture. They must see that they are rejecting the words of Christ, not our words.

I wrote earlier about the gospel encounter I had with a powerful businessman. When I asked him if he was a Christian, it didn't take me long to discern that his affirmative answer was not really a yes. He could label himself a Christian because he believed in the existence of a god. Again, though, it was clear in subsequent conversations that he had no belief in Jesus as Savior.

"I HAVE BEEN HURT BY THE CHURCH"

Church members can be cruel at times. They can be completely unaware of the effect their words have on new Christians and non-Christians. Almost every pastor has a story about a member of the church claiming ownership of a pew or row and asking a guest to move. Others can even be more pointed with their negativity.

When I was a pastor in St. Petersburg, Florida, people would show up for our services dressed in all sorts of ways. Not just the stereotypical Bermuda shorts and sandals of many Florida churchgoers. Some people's attire could be a bit extreme. I remember one young man who looked like he'd been rolled by a wave and then walked into our church straight from the beach. He was barefoot and wearing a ragged T-shirt that exposed more than it covered. His shorts were torn as well, and his hair was a tangled mop.

I was always proud of how our church members welcomed these guests. They greeted them warmly, invited them in, and sat with them. Some of these people might have been considered outcasts in other churches. The way our members embraced these "different sorts of folks" led several to become followers of Christ.

Sadly, too many non-Christians have stories of being hurt in churches. Sometimes it is a family member who has been hurt, but the pain is just as palpable. They have been targets of condescension and derision. They have been excluded from the "holy huddles."

You have a great opportunity to open a door for the gospel by treating someone well who has been hurt by a church or an individual Christian in the past. You can apologize on behalf of those who caused the pain, even if it happened somewhere else. Indeed, it might have been something that took place years ago in another state. But your humility in apologizing will often be well received. It certainly goes a long way toward demonstrating Christ's presence in your own life.

You can also explain gently that there are no perfect people in churches, only forgiven sinners. Indeed, the opportunity to share the gospel is often great when you acknowledge that the church is full of sinners who can be offensive to others.

A similar objection is that the church is full of hypocrites. Again, this objection can easily be turned into an opportunity. It's easy to affirm that many church members don't practice what they preach. You can even confess that you are one of them at times. But God is working to refine your character and make you more like Jesus. Such an honest admission can open the door for a conversation about the forgiveness and grace of Christ.

"HOW CAN I BELIEVE THE BIBLE IS TRUE?"

This objection may come in a number of forms. For example, the question may be phrased in a general way: How do I know the Bible is true? Doesn't the Bible have a lot of errors? How do you deal with all the contradictions in the Bible? How can you say that the writers of the Bible wrote a perfect book? Weren't they all just fallible humans?

The objection could also be voiced about specific verses or stories in the Bible. Volumes have been written on difficult sections of Scripture. Volumes have also been written on the statistical and historical evidence for the truthfulness of Scripture.

For years, I diligently read books by Norman Geisler and Josh McDowell, both of whom deal beautifully with apologetics in the books they have published.[9] Those books do a great job of defending the faith and demonstrating the veracity of Scripture. They are resources to which I will refer again and again. Still, I've found that I rarely need to use such apologetics in my gospel encounters. Often when someone questions the truthfulness of the Bible, they are simply trying to deflect the conversation.

There will certainly be times when you will need to research and provide detailed responses to people with specific questions or objections. You may deal with these issues more frequently in an academic environment, such as a college town. But most of the time, those to whom you speak will have deeper questions and deeper issues. When they ask specific questions about Bible passages or the truthfulness of Scripture, it is not unusual to find out later that they actually had other concerns.

It's also okay to admit you don't have an immediate answer if you aren't prepared to respond at the moment. In fact, it could give you an opportunity to set up another time to talk with that person. Between those conversations, God could very well be preparing the person even more.

Certainly, we need to be as prepared as possible to give a response when someone has a question or objection. Peter makes this clear in 1 Peter 3:15: "You must worship Christ as Lord of your life. And if someone asks about your hope as a believer, always be ready to explain it."

That passage is rightly used as an admonition to know the Bible and the truths of the faith so we can readily respond to questions. We indeed should be students of God's Word all of our lives. Still, the passage has an even deeper implication. The first sentence is clear. Our hearts must be right, and we must constantly demonstrate that we are living with Christ as Lord of our lives.

If there is any doubt, look at the verse that follows: "But do this in a gentle and respectful way. Keep your conscience clear. Then if people speak against you, they will be ashamed when they see what a good life you live because you belong to Christ" (1 Peter 3:16).

Several years ago, I engaged in gospel conversation for two years with one of the smartest people I've ever known. He constantly challenged my faith. He asked me difficult questions. Often I had to tell him that I didn't have an immediate answer. To be frank, I often felt inadequate and even embarrassed after our conversations.

The conversations became even more difficult when he interspersed his remarks with profanity. I knew he was testing me, and I prayed for a Christlike disposition toward him. I prayed that Christ would control my emotions. There were many days, however, that I felt pushed to the edge.

We ended up going our separate ways and moving to different cities, and I lost touch with him. Many years later, however, he tracked me down and called me. In the providence of God, we were once again living in the same city. He asked if he could come by my house. I was floored.

When he arrived, we took about thirty minutes to catch up on our lives. But then, true to his personality, he wanted to get to the point. This time there were no questions, no objections, and no profanity. He told me he wanted what I had. He wanted Jesus. And right there in my family room he became a follower of Christ.

My point is simple: Always be ready to defend the faith. Study the Bible diligently. Meditate on God's Word. But understand that, on this side of eternity, you will not have all the answers.

> Now we see things imperfectly, like puzzling reflections in a mirror, but then we will see everything with perfect clarity. All that I know now is partial and incomplete, but then I will know everything completely, just as God now knows me completely.
>
> I CORINTHIANS 13:12

We strive to learn. We strive to defend the faith. We strive to answer questions and respond to objections. Indeed, we strive to know all we can so we can respond well. But we know we will not have all the answers until we see Christ face to face. Until then, we strive to live lives that reveal Christ's presence in us. That kind of life can handle a lot of objections and answer a lot of questions.

THE ESSENCE OF IT ALL

I have often told my students and friends that we should be prepared and prayerful as we look for opportunities to share the gospel. Lately, however, I have reversed the sequence. I now say we are to be prayerful and prepared.

The change in order is not incidental. We must first be prepared in our hearts, and then in our heads.

The world is watching us. We have far more gospel opportunities than we realize. But the world is first looking for us to show love. That, in essence, is the greatest gospel conversation we can have.

Paul sums it perfectly in 1 Corinthians 13:13: "Three things will last forever—faith, hope, and love—and the greatest of these is love."

7

THREE BIG BARRIERS TO SHARING THE GOSPEL

There are certainly more than three barriers to sharing the gospel. Still, the three we're about to discuss are ones we hear regularly at Church Answers. We hear them from pastors and other church leaders who are convinced that *busyness*, *apathy*, and *lack of discipline* are "the big three."

Before we continue, however, let's return to the Great Commission for a moment and dig a little deeper to see what Jesus was saying:

Jesus came and told his disciples, "I have been given all authority in heaven and on earth. Therefore, go and make disciples of all the nations, baptizing them in the name of the Father and the Son and the

Holy Spirit. Teach these new disciples to obey all the commands I have given you. And be sure of this: I am with you always, even to the end of the age."

MATTHEW 28:18-20

Jesus opens and closes his statement with a promise of *power* and *presence*. We share the gospel under the authority of Christ. And his presence is with us "even to the end of the age." But what does Jesus tell us about sharing the gospel and making disciples?

First, let's look at the word *go*. The verb Jesus uses can also be translated "as you are going." Seen in this light, making disciples is something we do in our everyday walk of life. Sharing the gospel with ease should be part of our normal lifestyle.

A silly debate sometimes pops up over what the Great Commission really means. Is it *evangelism* or *discipleship*? Jesus makes it clear: It's *both*. We are to make disciples and baptize them. Baptism implies they are new converts. If they are new converts, then someone shared the gospel with them—which is evangelism.

But just as we wouldn't abandon a newborn baby to fend for itself, we don't leave new converts to their own devices. Instead, we teach, encourage, and equip them for ministry—which is the role of discipleship. Thus, as Jesus said, we must "teach these new disciples to obey all the commands I have given you."

The Great Commission is a statement of urgency. The task can't wait.

The Great Commission is a statement of priority. We are to make sure we are sharing the gospel as we go about our daily lives.

The Great Commission is a statement of discipline. Just as our physical bodies become weak and ineffective without physical exercise and nourishment, our spiritual bodies become weak and ineffective without the exercise of making disciples and the nourishment of God's Word.

If the Great Commission is among the last words Jesus spoke on earth, and every word oozes with urgency and priority, why are so few Christians eagerly obedient to it? Why is it often not our priority? These questions bring us to the three big barriers.

THE BARRIER OF BUSYNESS

I tried something new, and I'm not going back to the way things were.

More than a year ago, I decided to become a better steward of my time. To be honest, I usually do a decent job of getting my projects done. Obviously, I must have some level of discipline to have written thirty books. But before it starts to sound like I'm bragging about my wonderful stewardship of time, let me be transparent. Sometimes, I really stink at time management.

For example, in my younger years, when I was a husband and father, a full-time seminary student, a banker, and a pastor of a small church. I handled three of those major responsibilities pretty well. I bet you can guess where I fell short.

Yes, it was with my family. With a wife and three small sons, I was not at all consistent with my family time. All four of my family members suffered some level of neglect. I remembered and celebrated birthdays and anniversaries, and I rarely missed one of my boys' ball games, but I wasn't consistently available to them in the day-to-day.

When my boys were teenagers and I was traveling a lot, I decided to make them an offer. I gave them veto power over any of my speaking engagements. On top of that, I committed to taking my wife or one of my sons with me whenever possible when I traveled.

I kept my promise and we made a lot of good memories. In addition to a modest amount of international travel, Nellie Jo and I traveled to all fifty states.

But I forgot about the veto promise, the promise I'd made to cancel a trip if any one of my sons asked me to.

Well, I forgot, but one of my sons did not.

He called me into his room one night to talk. Such invitations were rare, so I knew it had to be serious.

"Dad," he began, "I really think you've been gone too much. Can you stay at home for a while?"

He was serious. It wasn't just a test. I responded by telling him I would cancel all my overnight trips for a month. His smile was one of contentment and relief.

Then I went to look at my calendar.

The next three weeks were fine. All speaking engagements were one-day trips, no overnight stays. Then I saw the fourth week.

Oh no.

Nellie Jo and I were headed to Hawaii for a speaking engagement.

So I went to my wife to discuss the matter with her. I figured she could help me rationalize the situation. I could keep my promise for three weeks, but we really should go to Hawaii, shouldn't we?

Her response was swift, and I should have expected it.

"Thomas," she said, both seriously and affectionately, "you made a promise to our sons. You have to keep it."

Sigh.

I was dean of a seminary then. I asked one of my professors if he would go to Hawaii in my stead.

He is still my friend today.

James 4:14 says, "How do you know what your life will be like tomorrow? Your life is like the morning fog—it's here a little while, then it's gone."

Moses prays in Psalm 90:12, "Teach us to realize the brevity of life, so that we may grow in wisdom."

Our lives are entrusted to us by God. We are to be good stewards of our time. We readily grasp the need for financial stewardship, but managing our time may be an even greater need. Jesus said, "Don't be so concerned about perishable things like food. Spend your energy seeking the eternal life that the Son of Man can give you. For God the Father has given me the seal of his approval" (John 6:27).

We are to focus our time on the eternal. Every person on earth will have an eternity—either in heaven or hell. Doesn't it seem obvious, then, that if we are too busy to share the gospel, we are simply too busy?

As part of my commitment to become a better steward of my time, I decided I would spend no more than thirty minutes a day on social media. I have no idea how much time I was spending on those sites before, but I'd wager it was a lot more than thirty minutes. Sadly, sometimes when I would get my Bible out to read, I would decide to "take just a few minutes" to check Facebook and Twitter, my two primary sites. Those "few minutes" often turned into several. And every minute I was on social media was one less minute invested in reading the Bible or praying.

I'm not so sure I really need those thirty minutes for social media. That's 182.5 hours a year or 7.6 days.

If I took 182 hours to share the gospel with 182 people for

one hour, what type of difference could God make through me? And I would still have a half hour remaining!

Here is the simple reality. If we don't have time to share the gospel with people, it's because we don't *make* time to share the gospel. And if we don't make time to share the gospel, it means we don't think sharing the gospel is all that important.

Though my words may seem harsh, please take them to heart. If evangelism is not a priority in our lives, it essentially means we don't care whether people go to heaven or hell. Those words apply just as forcefully to me as to you.

So, what can we do practically to solve our mythical problem of busyness? First, we can pray for opportunities to share the gospel. Obviously, that is not the first time you've read that encouragement in this book. It won't be the last time either. As God opens those doors for gospel conversations, take time to engage fully. You might have to spend less time on social media that day. You will be okay. I promise you will survive.

Here is something I started doing and plan to do more. I am posting a verse of Scripture on social media on a regular basis. If I'm going to spend time on social media, I might as well use it for God's glory. While posting a verse is not necessarily the same as a gospel conversation, it just might make a difference in someone's life. It might make an eternal difference.

You've heard testimonies to the power and efficacy of Scripture. Why not be a gospel bearer on social media through Bible verses? That would be a great way to spend your time. The writer of Hebrews reminds us, "The word of God is alive and powerful . . . , cutting between soul and spirit, between joint and marrow. It exposes our innermost thoughts and desires" (Hebrews 4:12).

What else can you do to spend more time sharing the gospel? Consider cultivating a friendship with someone you don't know or don't know well.

Let me be transparent again. This suggestion makes me uncomfortable. As an introvert, I dread initiating a relationship with someone. But like many other introverts, my preferred style of relating is one-on-one, and the more I get to know someone, the more comfortable I become. The first step might be difficult, but God didn't tell me to be comfortable. He told me to be obedient.

The matter of busyness is straightforward. The clock is the same for everyone. We all have twenty-four hours in a day. The issue is not that we don't have sufficient time. The issue is how we spend that time. The enemy would love for you to be too busy to share the gospel. In fact, he might be convincing you of that very lie right now.

It is a sin to be good when God has called you to be great. Our calendar can fill up with many good things. But are we making certain our calendar includes the great things, most notably the Great Commission?

We should never be too busy to share the gospel.

THE BARRIER OF APATHY

The barrier of apathy is a first cousin to the barrier of busyness. When we become too busy to share the gospel, we become apathetic to sharing the gospel. When we are apathetic about sharing the gospel, we fill our time with activities other than sharing the gospel.

Several years ago, I coauthored a book with my middle son, Art. The book was called *Raising Dad*. It was the story of what I did in raising my sons, and how well I did it—from Art's perspective.

In one chapter, we talk about quality time and quantity time spent with family members, in this case, a dad with a young son. Let me offer a word of caution: Art's memory of his childhood is selective. He remembers the best of me. I will give you my perspective after telling you his.

"Especially when I was younger," Art wrote, "when I knew nothing about the concept of 'quality time,' the amount of time spent with my father was far more important than what we did with that time. I wanted him to be there to sit and watch a football game, play catch, or visit my grandparents. I wanted to hang out at his office at church, sit in his lap, and play with our dogs."[10]

Art gave several examples of where he thought I had excelled at giving him time. He wrote about a long car trip the two of us made together. "Not many words were said on this trip," he recounted. "We were both pretty exhausted. If you had ridden along with us, you probably would have gone through several bouts of boredom, because the excitement of the journey was minimal. Yet, it is one of my favorite memories. We were together, and that was enough."[11]

In the second part of each chapter, I respond to Art. I had to be honest and transparent. I had to admit that I remembered far too many times when I wasn't there. I didn't want my children and (later) grandchildren living with a lie about their dad and granddad.

I was not always present. I did not always give Art, his brothers, and my wife the time they needed and deserved. I worked a lot. I worked too much. I'm ashamed of the busyness of my life at that time. And I still struggle with busyness today.

On the one hand, I could describe myself as an *absentee* father at many times in my life. That only means I wasn't there. But let's set the record straight. A better description would be that I was an *apathetic* father during those years. That adjective is much harsher, but more accurate. A parent who is in the military and must serve in another country away from home is an absentee parent. *Apathy*, though, describes motive and intent. It means you *could* do something, but you choose not to because it isn't important enough to you. Sadly, that described me as a dad to my young sons more times than I am comfortable admitting.

If we simply say we're not sharing the gospel and attach no reasons to the statement, we might leave the impression that we're doing something equally important. But if we're apathetic about sharing the gospel, our true motives are on display. We don't care enough about the gospel. We don't care about sharing the greatest news ever. We don't care that we are disobeying Jesus. We don't care about the eternity of those around us.

Do you get the sad and sordid picture?

If we're "too busy" for evangelism, it almost sounds acceptable. But if we just aren't motivated to share the gospel, we're clearly guilty of apathy. Our motives are not pure and right. We're confessing by our actions that we really don't care what Jesus says.

So how do we overcome this barrier? At risk of redundancy, we must *pray* about the condition of our hearts. We must *pray* for opportunities to share the gospel. We must *pray* for open eyes to see those opportunities.

We can also pray for a heart of compassion. Let's return to Matthew 9:36-38: "When [Jesus] saw the crowds, he had compassion on them because they were confused and helpless, like sheep without a shepherd. He said to his disciples, 'The harvest is great, but the workers are few. So pray to the Lord who is in charge of the harvest; ask him to send more workers into his fields.'"

The word *compassion* here means to feel something at a

gut level. You put yourself in someone else's shoes and you hurt for them. You have a burden to help them.

Jesus revealed his compassion for the lost by pleading for other workers to join him in the harvest fields. Simply stated, the lack of willing workers shows that not enough people have compassion. His prayer was for more workers, more people with compassion.

Perhaps our prayer should begin with our own hearts. Perhaps our prayer should be for our own compassion.

We can also overcome our apathy by spending time with lost people. When I went to Uganda and met the people of Kampala, I developed a love for them. The more I got to know them, the more that love grew. Today, Church Answers has a direct partnership with Ugandan churches to help train and equip more pastors. But in many ways my compassion for the Ugandans developed years earlier when I visited them.

Our love and compassion for people grows when we get to know them, when we spend time with them.

So how do we find the people we're supposed to reach? What do we say to them? How do we spend time together?

Without trying to be trite or flippant, I would simply say *trust God*. If you ask God for opportunities, if you include that prayer as a regular part of your prayer time with him, I have full confidence he will take care of connecting you with lost people. The context will make sense. The conversations will be natural. You will share the gospel with ease.

Take that first step. Tell God you are willing to be one of those workers in the harvest field.

Then see what he will do.

THE BARRIER OF A LACK OF DISCIPLINE

No doubt we will be talking for years to come about the pandemic that began in 2020. I was one of those optimists who believed the effects would be short-lived—maybe three or four months long. Yep, I really missed that one.

So, what did you do during the lockdown?

I wrote a book. But then, I've written a lot of books. So what was so different about writing a book during the pandemic? That's a story worth telling.

My publisher saw a lot of confusion in the Christian community and heard a lot of questions about where churches were headed as a result of the pandemic. They wanted to know if I could write a book quickly because the need was urgent.

So I wrote a book—in nineteen days!

Granted, the book was brief, not a major volume. Still, I had the discipline for that brief stretch to write *The Post-Quarantine Church*. (Yes, I can have discipline when I put my mind to it.)

Also in 2020, I splurged and bought a fitness treadmill, complete with a subscription for access to trainers around the world. I had never been a runner, but during the pandemic I became one at the age of sixty-five. (Did I mention I can have discipline when I put my mind to it?)

The words *discipline* and *disciple* come from the same root word, meaning "the right order" or "the right path." When parents discipline their children, they are trying to get them on the right path. When we say we are someone's disciple, we mean that we want to follow their path.

We sometimes refer to acts of deeper spirituality as "spiritual disciplines." We use those disciplines to set us on the right path. Some common spiritual disciplines include prayer; fasting; studying, reading, and meditating on Scripture; worship; stewardship; solitude; and gratitude.

Evangelism is a spiritual discipline as well. When we share the gospel, we demonstrate our desire to "get on the path" set forth by Jesus. We desire to be more like him. A disciple of Christ is one who follows him and practices the patterns of his life.

The Master Plan of Evangelism by Robert Coleman is one of the classic books on sharing the gospel.[12] The thesis is right there in the title. We should share the gospel in a disciplined and planned way, just as Jesus did.

What are some of the characteristics of an evangelistic discipline? Discipline begins with *commitment*. It's a cliché because it's true: You have to start somewhere.

When I first stepped onto my new treadmill, I remember

my apprehension about learning how to run, especially at my age. The recorded trainer that day was a guy named Tommy, from Portugal. As he began to lead me by video to the beaches and beautiful sites of his country, he said, "You have taken the hardest step. You have made a commitment to get on the treadmill to learn to run. Everything else will be easier from this point."

I'm not so sure that getting on the treadmill was the most difficult step. Tommy and the other trainers have led me through some pretty tough training sessions. But he was right that the first step was making a commitment to get on the treadmill. We began that first session running relatively slowly for only thirty seconds at a time. It took six weeks before I was running at a pace for thirty consecutive minutes.

Those who lack the discipline to share the gospel regularly have not taken the first step toward a longer-term commitment. One of the most common barriers to evangelism is simply the failure to make a commitment.

You remember O'Neal, the friend of my mentor Dr. Drummond, who became an ongoing illustration of sharing the gospel? O'Neal was described by those who knew him as "an evangelism machine." But he didn't start out that way. He started by making a commitment. Then, after months of practicing the discipline of sharing the gospel, it became more natural for him. But it took commitment and perseverance to get to that point.

The first step toward overcoming a lack of discipline is simply to make a heartfelt decision to share the gospel. Make a commitment.

The second step is to be *ready* to share the gospel when the opportunity arises. Again, I am convinced that God will give you opportunities when you make the commitment.

Though it happened several years ago, I still vividly remember how God opened one particular door for me. I had committed myself to become more disciplined in sharing the gospel. In fact, I prayed for opportunities the same night I made the commitment.

The next morning, I was flying to a speaking engagement. At the airport, I passed a person who asked if I wanted my shoes shined. I declined politely. I will never be nominated for "best dressed," and my dingy, scuffed shoes were fine with me.

But as I passed the shoeshine station, I felt nudge to turn around and go back. Was this God's Spirit telling me I had an open door? I let the man know I had changed my mind. He took one look at my shoes and told me that was a good decision.

Within minutes, Michael and I were having a spiritual conversation. Frankly, I don't remember how it began. I know I didn't force the issue. God opened the door and gave me the opportunity. After that, I made a point of visiting

Michael every time I went to the airport. Because I traveled often, he and I were able to have several conversations.

I'm hesitant to share the next part of the story, lest I seem like one of the hypocrites that Jesus criticizes in Matthew 6:2 for "blowing trumpets . . . to call attention to their acts of charity." Nevertheless, it's an important part of my open-door story, so I'll take the risk.

First, I tipped Michael generously. God has blessed me many times financially, and I enjoy blessing others as a result. Michael never had an attitude of presumption; he was always grateful.

Second, on one occasion he told me about a death in his family. I think it was his grandmother. When I asked if he was going to the funeral, he casually responded that he couldn't really afford to fly there. He was neither hinting nor expecting a response from me. He was simply responding to my question.

After he finished shining my shoes, I went to the nearest ATM and withdrew a sum of cash. Then I went back to Michael and handed it to him. I told him I wanted him to go to his grandmother's funeral.

There were no words. He looked at me for a moment and then excused himself and made a dash to the men's room. He couldn't afford to cry on the job. I left with a song in my heart.

A few weeks later, Michael told me he had become a

Christian. He had found a church near his home and was already connecting with other Christians.

I have no idea what other influences and people God put in Michael's path. I simply rejoiced that he was a believer in Jesus. But I am grateful God used me the way he did. I had asked him for an opportunity. I had made a commitment. And I had done my best to show the love of Christ to Michael in what I said and what I did.

Habits develop when we practice a discipline with commitment and regularity. The habit of evangelism grows from first making a commitment and then asking God to open doors for sharing the gospel.

I continue to be amazed at how God works, even though by now I really should come to anticipate it. God gives us the opportunities. He teaches us to speak with ease about the gospel. He gives us the words. And often his Spirit convicts others of their need to receive the Savior who will forgive them and give them eternal life.

UNDERSTANDING THE WHY OF THE BARRIERS

Lately, I find myself reading Joshua 1 over and over. During the time of Moses, the Israelites had balked at entering the Promised Land. As a consequence, they had wandered in the wilderness of the Sinai Peninsula for forty years. Most of the adults who had escaped from Egypt never got to the new land. They died during the wandering. They had been too fearful to venture into the new land, though God had promised to protect them.

The desert was not a hospitable place. It was harsh and devoid of water and vegetation, except in oases and wadis. Still, God provided. He supplied them with water and food. He provided safety and guidance. But the people did not believe he would take care of them on the other side of the Jordan River. They paid a heavy price for their disobedience.

In contrast, Joshua 1 is full of hope. The God of fresh chances is giving the Israelites another opportunity to enter the Promised Land. He has appointed Joshua as their new leader in the aftermath of Moses' death. It is time to trust God. It is time to enter.

God repeats the promises he made to Moses: "Wherever you set foot, you will be on land I have given you. . . . No one will be able to stand against you. . . . For I will be with you. . . . I will not fail you or abandon you" (Joshua 1:3, 5).

Then God gives Joshua a commandment—"Be strong and courageous" (Joshua 1:6)—which he repeats in verse 9: "This is my command—be strong and courageous! Do not be afraid or discouraged. For the LORD your God is with you wherever you go."

So, what does this have to do with sharing the gospel? Simply stated, God has promised us his presence and we have responded with a lack of faith. We have so many potential objections. What if I offend someone? What if they reject me? What if they don't want to listen? What if I mess up what I'm supposed to say?

Each and every objection reveals that we are not trusting God to be with us, to empower us, and to prepare the way for us. The bottom line is that we lack faith.

The Israelites remembered what it meant to lack faith. Many of them had been children during the wilderness years, but they remembered. At the very least, they had heard the stories repeatedly. When Moses had said it was time to enter the Promised Land, the people could only see the obstacles. They saw fortified cities and fierce warriors who could kill them.

But now God was giving them another opportunity. This time, under the leadership of Joshua, they entered the Promised Land.

When we are apathetic about sharing the gospel, when we lack faith in God, we don't really believe he will lead us into greater areas than we've ever known. We somehow believe that remaining silent about our faith will lead to a more fulfilling life than being ready to speak for Jesus.

When we have doubts and fears about sharing the gospel, we betray our lack of faith in God. But remember what God told Joshua: "This is my command—be strong and courageous! Do not be afraid or discouraged. For the LORD your God is with you wherever you go."

Remember the Great Commission in Matthew 28:18-20, where Jesus reminds his followers that they will be going under his authority, and where he promises he will be with them wherever they go.

Remember the Great Commission in Acts 1:8, where Jesus tells his "sent ones" that they will have the power of the Holy Spirit.

It's simple but powerful. Jesus commands us to go, and he gives us everything we need. Any barrier in our hearts and minds is there because we lack faith. It's time to end the excuses. It's time to stop focusing on the barriers. It's time to claim the promise of Jesus' power and presence. It's time to stop focusing on what we cannot do and start looking at what Jesus can do.

The message is clear.

It's time to go.

8

WHEN THEY BECOME CHRISTIANS

I chuckle at the title of this book, *Sharing the Gospel with Ease*, in the context of my own first stumbling attempt at evangelism. When I tried to share the gospel with my friend Jim, I didn't come close to being at ease. I was scared to death. But I learned an important lesson, one that I now take with me every day: God preceded me in that encounter, and he was with me in that encounter.

If my eloquence or calm demeanor were prerequisites for Jim becoming a Christian, he would have gone unreached. I fumbled my words. I was a nervous wreck. God used me anyway.

Decades later, I still look back on that day with amazement. Through the power of God and the presence of the

Holy Spirit, Jim became a Christian. His decision did not depend on me. God took control. God is always in control. Recognizing that one simple fact may be what it takes to help you share the gospel with ease.

But there's another, equally important part to Jim's story. Not only did he become a *believer* in Christ; he also became a close *disciple* of Christ's. At the risk of further redundancy, I will say it again: Jim embodies the intended result of the Great Commission. He became Christ's disciple.

We simply must not see Matthew 28:18-20 as a dichotomy. It is not conversion *or* discipleship. It is conversion *and* discipleship. The Great Commission is a progression. We share the gospel so the Spirit can convict people of their sin and make them believers. We continue to share the gospel so that new believers become devoted followers of Christ.

Jim was not a one-and-done Christian. (That's an oxymoron for sure.) He still needed to mature as a believer. Over time, the work of the Spirit in his life became evident. He immersed himself in the Bible. He prayed with consistency and anticipation. He yielded to the work of God in his life to clean up past sinful patterns and create new patterns of holiness.

And Jim became active—very active—in his church. He did not view this work as a legalistic obligation. He served in the church with joy.

To be clear, Jim developed personal spiritual disciplines.

But he also developed corporate spiritual disciplines. Both are critical to our growth in Christ.

PERSONAL SPIRITUAL DISCIPLINES

Most resources on growing as a Christian focus on personal spiritual disciplines. For example, many new Christians are encouraged to read the Gospel of John as a starting point for understanding the Bible. Then they are often pointed to a plan for reading the Bible in its entirety.

Indeed, we cannot overemphasize the importance for new believers to get into the Word. Brad Waggoner, in his study of spiritual disciplines in *The Shape of Faith to Come*, finds that daily Bible reading is the number one correlated factor to growth in other disciplines.[13] Simply stated, the more we read the Bible with consistency, the more likely we are to have a disciplined prayer life, share the gospel, and maintain consistency in other spiritual disciplines.

Prayer, for certain, is key to growing as a Christian. We will hear from God as we immerse ourselves in the Bible. And we will hear from God and speak to God as we develop a more consistent prayer life.

As we pray, we praise God for who he is. Our prayer lives are thus a doxology. We confess our sins. Though our sins—past, present, and future—have been forgiven through Christ's death on the cross, we break fellowship with him when we sin. In other words, our relationship is secure, but our fellowship can be broken. We confess our sins to restore fellowship.

We also thank God for the innumerable blessings he has given us. We intercede for others when we pray. I have learned to record prayer requests in a prayer app on my smartphone so I don't forget to pray for others.

We pray for our own needs as well. Though we don't want our prayer time to become a shopping list of our own needs, God takes joy when we present our needs, burdens, and concerns to him. He rejoices when we ask him in faith.

We should pray as well for opportunities to share the gospel. Evangelism is a spiritual discipline that should not be neglected. Opportunities to share the gospel will become more abundant and apparent when we ask God for open doors and open eyes.

Personal spiritual disciplines are vitally important for believers to grow in Christ. Paul told Timothy to focus his life on spiritual disciplines: "Do not waste time arguing over godless ideas and old wives' tales. Instead, train yourself to be godly" (1 Timothy 4:7). The key is to become more godly; our ultimate goal is to be like Christ. But notice that the text says we are to train *ourselves*. Spiritual disciplines are to be a personal priority.

There are many spiritual disciplines for us to master: praying, fasting, meditating on Scripture, worshiping, and serving, to name just a few. The key is to practice these disciplines with joy and consistency. As we do, we are like an athlete training himself or herself. Just as an athlete becomes physically stronger, quicker, and faster with training, we become more like Christ as we train ourselves spiritually.

OFTEN-NEGLECTED CORPORATE DISCIPLINES

Countless books and other resources have been created to help people grow spiritually through individual disciplines. Indeed, many resources focus exclusively on individual disciplines. Some may give a nod to *corporate* disciplines, but the reference often reads something like this: "You should get involved in a local church where you can be connected to other Christians."

Though I would never suggest that we should minimize our personal disciplines, we cannot afford to ignore or neglect the corporate spiritual disciplines. By "corporate disciplines," I mean areas of spiritual growth that happen in the context of the local church, in the presence of other Christians.

The great majority of the New Testament was written to or about local churches. From Acts 2, the birth of the first church at Jerusalem, through Revelation 1–3, where we read seven letters to seven churches, we learn about growth and obedience in the context of the local church.

We sometimes forget that many of the Epistles and the

seven letters in Revelation were written to very specific churches, at very specific times, addressing very specific issues. Understanding the particular context can help us understand the more broadly applicable principles in these letters.

For example, when we quote Romans 3:23—"Everyone has sinned; we all fall short of God's glorious standard"—it can be helpful to understand that Paul was teaching the members of the church in Rome about the magnificence of God's grace.

Likewise with verses such as Philippians 4:13, where we learn about Christ's power in our lives: "I can do everything through Christ, who gives me strength." Again, Paul is writing to a specific church—in the Roman colony of Philippi. The encouraging words we memorize and study today were encouraging words written personally to a well-loved church in a very specific location.

It's no coincidence, then, that our growth as Christians should be in the context, fellowship, and accountability of the local church. Even the New Testament books that are letters written to specific individuals—such as Timothy, Titus, or Philemon—are mostly about matters in the local church. The pastoral letters, for example, deal with major organizational issues in local churches.

Likewise, the letter to the Hebrews, which does not name a specific location, and whose authorship is debated, nevertheless clearly defines its audience as Christians who are in fellowship with one another: "And so, dear brothers and sisters who belong to God and are partners with those called to heaven . . ." (Hebrews 3:1).

There is little doubt that God, in his divine plan, intends for Christians to grow in the context and accountability of the local church. Therefore, when we evangelize, we seek to make disciples *and* connect them to a local church.

THE TWO BIG INSTITUTIONS OF THE BIBLE

The New Testament clearly focuses on two God-ordained institutions: *the family* and *the church*. For example, 1 Timothy and 1 Peter both interweave important admonitions about church and family. We all have specific roles and responsibilities to carry out in each of these groups.

Yet how many times have you heard someone say they aren't involved in a local church because it is full of hypocrites? Indeed, no local church is perfect. In fact, no individual member in a church is perfect either. The observation is true. Churches are full of sinners forgiven by the grace of our Lord Jesus Christ. We are a gathering of hypocrites in the process of transformation. In the meantime, we may often act contrary to our own beliefs.

But hypocrisy can't be a barrier to belonging. Look at the institution of the family. Families are full of people who say one thing and do another. If hypocrisy were sufficient reason, no one would have a family to love, nurture, and enjoy. There are no perfect families, nor perfect family members. That includes you and me and our clans. But does that keep us from belonging to them? From participating in our families? Absolutely not! Nor should hypocrisy be an excuse to keep us from belonging to a church family.

We must do everything we can to incorporate believers into the local church. Many Christians bemoan the lack of discipleship today, but the New Testament has a clear plan. Most discipleship takes place in a local congregation. For new believers, joining a local church is not merely a postscript to their decision or a simple step toward maturing in Christ; it is the single most important thing a believer can do.

The New Testament is unequivocal about this issue. You cannot adequately mature in Christ outside the fellowship and accountability of the local church. Simply stated, the New Testament knows nothing of true discipleship outside the fellowship of the church.

FELLOWSHIP IN THE LOCAL CHURCH

The book of Acts begins with Jesus' ascension and then Peter's sermon at Pentecost in Acts 2. When Peter concludes his sermon, about three thousand people accept Christ as their Lord and Savior.

Jerusalem naturally becomes the location of the first local church. In Acts 2:42-47, we see a description of this first church, which serves as a model for other churches to follow.

Acts 2:42 demonstrates the close connection these believers had to one another: "All the believers devoted themselves to the apostles' teaching, and to fellowship, and to sharing in meals (including the Lord's Supper), and to prayer." The first church comprised a gathering of believers who were dedicated to each other and to the local church. The text is clear that they devoted themselves to fellowship and the sharing of meals and the Lord's Supper together.

From the inception of this first church, there was no sense that joining together was optional. They had a deep and unwavering commitment to each other individually and to the church corporately. The first step in discipleship was clear and unequivocal: They joined a local church.

We mustn't overlook or downplay this foundational principle of discipleship. In committing themselves to the fellowship of believers, these new Christians were making a clear statement about putting others before themselves. A healthy church is one where the members don't ask what the church can do for them. Instead, they ask how they can serve God through the ministry of the church.

All the believers met together in one place and shared everything they had. They sold their property and possessions and shared the money with those in need. They worshiped together at the Temple each day, met in homes for the Lord's Supper, and shared their meals with great joy and generosity—all the while praising God and enjoying the goodwill of all the people. And each day the Lord added to their fellowship those who were being saved.

ACTS 2:44-47

God's plan here is unmistakable. By placing believers in fellowship with one another, he meant to establish a dynamic in which people would not be focused on their own preferences and desires. In a healthy church, as in a healthy family, members look after one another's needs. That is precisely what it means to say that the believers devoted themselves to fellowship. They began growing in Christ by subordinating their own needs to the needs of others. They immediately began practicing the "one another" principle that is repeated throughout much of the New Testament.[14]

TEACHING IN THE LOCAL CHURCH

Believers grow in Christ by immersing themselves in the teachings of Scripture. Though the canon of Scripture had not yet been fully developed in the first century, it is clear that these early Christians were devoting themselves to the teachings of Christ and the Old Testament.

These new believers were taught the truths of Scripture by the apostles, in both a larger worship context at the Temple and in smaller meetings in homes, where they also celebrated the Lord's Supper (Acts 2:46).

This example can be seen as both descriptive and prescriptive. One of the major ways to grow in maturity as Christians is by immersing ourselves in the Word in both larger and smaller contexts. In most churches today, we refer to the larger context as a *worship service*, and we identify the smaller context by a number of names, including small groups, home groups, Sunday school classes, community groups, life groups, and others.

And though we can certainly worship and study Scripture with others in a variety of ways and places, we typically find greater regularity and accountability in a local congregation. It is with that imperfect institution, that place where forgiven hypocrites come together, that we can best be devoted to God's teachings.

We grow in Christ as we learn more about him. God gave us local congregations as places where we can learn with devotion together.

PRAYER IN THE LOCAL CHURCH

Recently, I've been teaching in a community group at the church where I'm a member. Before I introduce the lesson each week, we pause for a time of prayer. We often pray for our physical needs. We pray for an unemployed member to find a job. We pray for the salvation of a member's father. We pray for a member who is going through stress at work. We pray for opportunities to share the gospel and invite others to church.

We have seen many prayers answered. At times, we have been amazed by the power of God.

Though I'm not always amazed at these prayer times, I realize I should be. Every person in that community group exhibits interdependence and vulnerability by asking for prayer. Each one demonstrates tremendous faith by talking to God in prayer.

In our worship services on Sundays, we pray together as a church. From the inception of our church, prayer has been an integral part of our services. Praying is neither rote nor routine. Our pastor, who happens to be one of my sons, kneels at the front almost every service during our corporate prayer times. More often than not, several people lay their hands on him and pray for him.

Sure, we can pray on our own—and we should. Personal prayer is a spiritual discipline I will not neglect. But there is something extraordinary, something truly supernatural when the church comes together to pray.

I thank God that I am a member of a church that prays together, that values prayer, and puts a priority on prayer.

Such should be the pattern of every church. I do not take for granted those times when our church prays together.

I wonder if the Holy Spirit specifically led Luke to mention prayer as the final word in Acts 2:42:

> All the believers devoted themselves to the apostles' teaching, and to fellowship, and to sharing in meals (including the Lord's Supper), *and to prayer* [emphasis added].

It seems that prayer was a foundational and powerful reality in the Jerusalem church. And look at the result: "A deep sense of awe came over them all, and the apostles performed many miraculous signs and wonders" (Acts 2:43). The primacy of prayer was followed by "a deep sense of awe" and a manifestation of God's power.

Christians should always be actively engaged in a local church. Ultimately, growth in Christ cannot happen apart from a local congregation. The gathering of believers is central and important to the process. Among the many reasons we join a local church is the awesome opportunity to pray together with other believers. As we pray together, we collectively demonstrate our dependence on God and our trust in him.

WORSHIP IN THE LOCAL CHURCH

Worship is a spiritual discipline, both in a personal and corporate sense. In Acts 2:46, we are reminded that in the first church "they worshiped together at the Temple each day." When Luke wrote these words, under the inspiration of the Holy Spirit, he was careful to include the word *together*. In the context of belonging to a church, worship takes place with others. It is indeed a together function.

What is fascinating in the concluding verses of Acts 2 is seeing corporate worship turn into evangelism. As people outside the church observed the worship of these new Christians, they were amazed by the power and unity that was evident among the believers. And while the believers were "praising God and enjoying the goodwill of all the people" (verse 46), something amazing happened: "Each day the Lord added to their fellowship those who were being saved" (verse 47).

Recently a man walked into the church where I'm a member. He had no means of transportation or even a driver's license. He was just walking down the street and God prompted him to walk into our church building. He was amazed by the worship service, and he was convicted by the Holy Spirit.

And the Lord added him to our fellowship as one who was saved.

Believers in general, and new believers in particular, must connect with a local church. One of the primary ways for believers to grow as disciples is by connecting to a congregation and worshiping together. It was the pattern of the early church, and it should be our pattern today.

GENEROSITY IN THE LOCAL CHURCH

Believers who belong to a local church should also practice the spiritual discipline of generosity, or stewardship. Luke focuses heavily on the generosity of the first church: "All the believers met together in one place and shared everything they had. They sold their property and possessions and shared the money with those in need" (Acts 2:44-45).

Generosity is a clear mark of a disciple of Christ. And it is best expressed in the context of the local church. Acts 2 makes it abundantly clear that generosity isn't limited to money. The followers of Christ were eager to sell their own possessions and give to others. They had a lifestyle of giving that extended from the church to the home: "They . . . shared their meals with great joy and generosity" (Acts 2:46).

The spiritual discipline of generosity, like other spiritual disciplines, can be practiced in both singular and corporate settings. But when generosity is practiced among believers in the church, the result is both encouragement and accountability. As one person gives abundantly, others are inspired to give generously as well. And in a joyful sense, this "together generosity" engenders accountability to one another.

The first church members did not merely give; they gave abundantly, sacrificially, and joyfully.

WHY THE LOCAL CHURCH REALLY MATTERS IN EVANGELISM

In my community group at church, we have good times of fellowship and good conversations about inviting people to church and sharing the gospel. I am always encouraged by the desire of my fellow believers to tell others about Christ. My church and community group are microcosms of how to help believers become more effective at sharing the gospel with ease.

It may seem as if this final chapter in a book on evangelism has taken a strange turn. I started with issues related to sharing the gospel and moved on to the importance of the local church. I hope you see the vital connection between the two.

The Great Commission is about making disciples. For most of the New Testament, disciple-making takes place in a local congregation. As people became followers of Christ, one of the keys to their becoming fruit-bearing disciples was to connect with a local church.

To be clear, connecting with a local church is not merely

an addendum to conversion. It is much more than merely suggesting that a new Christian should find a church in his or her area. Becoming an active participant in a local congregation is vital to disciple-making.

In many churches today, membership has become optional. And the expectations of members are minimal. Involvement in a local church has become more like membership in a civic club or country club. It's nice to be there to get the perks and benefits, but active participation is certainly not required.

That type of attitude is foreign to the New Testament vision of the church. Connection to and involvement in a local congregation is vital to our growth and maturity as disciples of Christ.

You have read my testimony throughout this book. Allow me to connect some dots. As you remember, my football coach, Joe Hendrickson, shared the gospel with me after practice one day. It seemed so effortless and so natural on his part. Indeed, he could be the poster child for sharing the gospel with ease.

I was a teenager when I became a Christian. Do you know how I began to mature spiritually after my conversion? Well, to be honest, I really did not mature much at all at first. I continued to live a rebellious life in both high school and college. I suppose that anyone who observed me during those days would have concluded that I was not a Christian.

But I was. I had repented of past sins and placed my faith in Jesus Christ. I know with total conviction that I received the grace of salvation on that day when Coach Joe shared the gospel with me.

But then what happened to me?

With the wisdom of experience and the clarity of hindsight, I know the answer. I didn't get connected with a local church. And though it's not intended as an excuse, there wasn't much to attract me to go to church at the time. The church where my parents had been members all my life had split not once but twice. And many of the other churches in the community were also in turmoil.

But I still should have connected with a church. Instead, I did just the opposite. I dropped out of church altogether. I became an unchurched Christian as a teenager. I didn't attend worship services. I wasn't in a small group. I had no one to hold me accountable for my spiritual growth. I acted more like an unsaved person than many unsaved people.

That changed, however, shortly after I got married. My wife gently nudged me to get into a church. And when she became pregnant with our first child, her nudging took on a bit of urgency. She wasn't nagging me by any stretch of the imagination, but she was determined that our children would grow up in the nurture of a local church.

I had the same conviction, so I willingly—if not

eagerly—went with her to visit churches in our area. We ultimately found a home at a church in our neighborhood.

Then it happened. My spiritual growth had been stunted for so long that I was shocked to see how quickly God began to work in my life. Those who knew me were amazed at the change in my life. My own mother expressed concern that I was going overboard instead of growing more methodically as a believer.

But once I became involved in a loving and active congregation, I couldn't get enough of church life. I loved my pastor. I loved the worship services. I loved my Sunday school class. I was finally part of a family of believers who loved me, nurtured me, and held me accountable. It was one of the most precious times of my life.

Of course, I learned as time went on that my church wasn't perfect. No church is. Still, it was disappointing to discover that some of my fellow church members did not live exemplary spiritual lives. There was inconsistency, even hypocrisy. But God used that imperfect church to mold me—far from perfect myself—into a person who desired to walk with Christ. In essence, I moved from being a mere convert to becoming a disciple.

Whatever influence I've had on others becoming Christians had its beginning in that church. I can honestly say that nothing in my life was headed toward discipleship until I connected with the local church.

We are called to share the gospel. We are called to make disciples. And though the title of this book may seem impossible to some, we should be sharing our faith with such consistency that it becomes natural—or should I say supernatural?—to share the gospel with ease.

I noted earlier my life verse, Acts 4:20: "We cannot stop telling about everything we have seen and heard." These were the words spoken by Peter and John, facing further imprisonment, punishment, and even death, after being commanded by the "rulers and elders and teachers of religious law" (Acts 4:5) in Jerusalem "never again to speak or teach in the name of Jesus" (Acts 4:18).

Peter and John did not respond with a rebellious, "We will not." No, they responded with the powerful statement, "We *cannot*." Jesus Christ was so real and so powerful to them—they had seen and heard so much—that they simply could not stop talking about him. They not only shared the gospel with ease, they shared it with unhindered enthusiasm and urgency.

Evangelism is absent in many Christians. It is weak in many others. We have become so busy doing "good things" that we are neglecting the best thing.

It's time to change that.

It's time for Christians to stop yielding to the quiet lies of Satan, who tells us our silence is okay, that evangelism is for some Christians, but not all.

It's time for you and me to spread the Good News and make disciples wherever we go.

It's time for a revival of evangelism.

I pray God will let it begin in you and me.

NOTES

1. Thom S. Rainer, *The Book of Church Growth: History, Theology, and Principles* (Nashville, TN: Broadman Press, 1993), 14–15.
2. C. S. Lewis, *Mere Christianity* (London: Collins, 1952), 54–56.
3. For all this and more, see my book *The Post-Quarantine Church* (Carol Stream, IL: Tyndale Momentum, 2020).
4. George C. Wallace, first inaugural address, January 14, 1963, Montgomery, Alabama, 8:00–8:07, https://speakola.com/political /george-wallace-segregation-now-inaugural-speech-1963.
5. For more, see my book *The Unchurched Next Door* (Grand Rapids, MI: Zondervan), 2003).
6. D. James Kennedy, *Evangelism Explosion* (Carol Stream, IL: Tyndale), 1996.
7. "Death Rate Is 120 per Minute," Bioethics Research Library, Kennedy Institute of Ethics, Georgetown University, accessed June 14, 2021, https://bioethics.georgetown.edu/2016/04/death-rate-is-120-per -minute/.
8. See Jonathan Merritt, "Oprah Finds Reasons to Believe," *The Atlantic*, October 18, 2015, https://www.theatlantic.com/politics/archive/2015 /10/oprah-finds-reasons-to-believe/411151/.
9. See, for instance, Norman Geisler, *I Don't Have Enough Faith to Be an Atheist* (Wheaton, IL: Crossway, 2004) and Josh McDowell, *More Than a Carpenter* (Carol Stream, IL: Tyndale, 1977, 2004).

10. Thom S. Rainer and Art Rainer, *Raising Dad: What Fathers and Sons Learn from Each Other* (Nashville, TN: B&H, 2007), 126–27.
11. Rainer and Rainer, *Raising Dad*, 127.
12. Robert E. Coleman, *The Master Plan of Evangelism*, 2nd ed. (Grand Rapids, MI: Spire, 2010).
13. Brad J. Waggoner, *The Shape of Faith to Come: Spiritual Formation and the Future of Discipleship* (Nashville, TN: B&H, 2008), 68.
14. For a list of the fifty-nine "one another" passages in the New Testament, see http://storage.cloversites.com/wakarusamissionarychurch/documents/59one_another_scriptures.pdf.

ABOUT THE AUTHOR

Thom S. Rainer is the founder and CEO of Church Answers. With nearly forty years of ministry experience, Thom has spent a lifetime committed to the growth and health of the local church and its leaders. He has been a pastor of four churches and interim pastor of ten churches, as well as a best-selling author, popular speaker, professor, and dean. He is a graduate of the University of Alabama and earned an MDiv and PhD from The Southern Baptist Theological Seminary. Rainer has written numerous books, including three that ranked as number one bestsellers: *I Am a Church Member*, *Autopsy of a Deceased Church*, and *Simple Church*. He and his wife live in Nashville.